Historic Review of the Order of the Knights Hospitallers of St. John of Jerusalem, of Rhodes, and Malta

William Henry Lannin

Nabu Public Domain Reprints:

You are holding a reproduction of an original work published before 1923 that is in the public domain in the United States of America, and possibly other countries. You may freely copy and distribute this work as no entity (individual or corporate) has a copyright on the body of the work. This book may contain prior copyright references, and library stamps (as most of these works were scanned from library copies). These have been scanned and retained as part of the historical artifact.

This book may have occasional imperfections such as missing or blurred pages, poor pictures, errant marks, etc. that were either part of the original artifact, or were introduced by the scanning process. We believe this work is culturally important, and despite the imperfections, have elected to bring it back into print as part of our continuing commitment to the preservation of printed works worldwide. We appreciate your understanding of the imperfections in the preservation process, and hope you enjoy this valuable book.

A HISTORY OF
MALTA KNIGHTHOOD

SIR W. HENRY LANNIN

A Historic Review of the Order of the Knights Hospitallers of St. John of Jerusalem, of Rhodes, and Malta

WITH A CLEAR AND AUTHORITATIVE ACCOUNT OF THE ORDER'S FOUNDING, ITS MARVELOUS ACHIEVEMENTS THROUGHOUT CENTURIES, ITS KINSHIP AND CO-OPERATION WITH THE KNIGHTS OF THE TEMPLE, TOGETHER WITH AN ILLUMINATING SURVEY OF THE MOVEMENTS OF NATIONS AND THEIR RELIGIOUS IMPULSES AND PREJUDICES

BY
SIR W. HENRY LANNIN

BOSTON
THE FOUR SEAS COMPANY
PUBLISHERS

Copyright, 1922, by
W. Henry Lannin

The Four Seas Press
Boston, Mass., U.S.A.

PREFATORY

AS every tree which adorns the surface of the earth has upsprung from a vegetative seed which to man's eye was hidden, in like manner has every visible institution, of whatever nature or formative mould, upsprung from some germinal source, and, very generally, the initial source remains largely unknown, as also, it may be, of slight interest to many who view with gratifying zest and who take membership interest in the increasing popularity of the working institution. Though mankind's numerous institutions,—be they good, bad, or indifferent,—have their roots deeply imbedded in the soil of the historic past of men's movements, struggles, philanthropic activities, yet we may well opine that whatsoever zeal and impelling motive they possessed they had no foreview as to their having founded an institution which in time's onflow would grow into international proportions. However, as "great oaks from little acorns grow," so it is an evolutionary law that "first the blade, then the ear, then the full corn in the ear." Manifestly enough, by the law of from the lesser to the greater, every human institution has materialized. Moreover, the ever-extending bane or blessing outwardly functioned by each society, institution, and Order under the sun invariably bears, in a greater or lesser measure, the nature and essence of the germinal root. True, there may have come upon the institutional tree some blight which has perverted and paralyzed it to such an extent as to evilly affect in stock, limb, and twig, but in spite of such calamitous event there still inheres a latent root principle which when possibly revitalized—if, indeed, the initial force was of serviceable worth—will again manifest to ennobling results. Then, also, as the on-sweep of centuries goes to the change of manners, customs, and mode of living,—all ever keeping step with the times, be they what they may,— it follows that no ancient institution which continues to exist can in wisdom function in the same manner as of former centuries. Writing as to revision and change of method by institutions, a historian has aptly said, "The general principles of the religious societies of knighthood fitted themselves to the times like the chain-mail, which was flexible to all the motions of the body." Changed conditions demand a revision of method, if not of spirit. However, it is well to consider that institutions which in their sourcing possessed universal and time-lasting principles of morality, humanitarianism, and ennobling virtues—such as were incorporated into the fabric of the Order of St. John—cannot indifferently depart and drift therefrom without being blighted with the foul stigma of degeneracy.

Then, also, it is quite possible for officials to incessantly and loudly laud the heroism, unselfish zeal, and nobleness of an institution's founders, while they themselves as members do but play the puritanical role. It is folly, yes, brazen presumption, to maintain that the virtuous lives and deeds of an institution's founders is evidence of the continued purity of the institution. If individual men, throughout each passing century, were imbued with the same mind—like unto beavers and bees—such might reasonably be, but the thoughts of men change with the years. Only measurably does the warp and woof of an institution mould and temper its members. There ever exist individual differences and dispositions, some good, true, and of sterling worth, others ever tending to weed-croppings and unjust conduct. With the proffering of this philosophic sheaf, the author of this treatise will endeavor to set before the reader's mind a historic review of the amazing deeds, prowess, as also the motives and customs of the renowned Order of St. John of Jerusalem, of Cyprus, Rhodes, and Malta. In America this knightly Order is professedly working as a lineal descendant of the Scotch-English Branch, constituting the Sixth *Langue* (language) of the old Institution. The historic contents of this treatise has been made possible to the author's pen by his being privileged to study the writings of the standard European and English treatises which voluminously set forth every phase of the Order.

The task taken in hand was no light one, but not an hour passed but what gave mental interest to the author. Not possessing the rare publications, the writer was generously supplied with the necessary volumes by his knightly friend and well wisher, Sir Frederic H. Willson, P.G.C., Grand Recorder of the Order's commanderies in Massachusetts, Rhode Island, and Connecticut, who at no small expenditure of money and searchings has secured from abroad invaluable literature. Thus it is that this treatise contains the very cream of authoritative statement relative to this Order, "the venerable patriarch of European chivalry."

It is the author's conviction that quite often is it true that some minor incident in a man's, or, it may be, a body of men's, passing days has, like a bubble on flowing waters, gained attention, whereas the serviceable waters in their flowing have slightly awakened mind interest. Thus it is that if one would rightly appraise an institution which serviceably functions, and for seven centuries did unceasingly function, among men, the proper course to take is to enlighten the mind as to its historic activities and, if it be possible, trace it to its source. Of course, this will mean some vigorous mental touring, yet the tour will be of life lasting and mind illuminating value to the voyager.

PREFATORY

As a closing prefatory word: While of ready and charitable mind both author and reader must in forbearance throw a generous mantle over the many deeds of those men who in the blood-heating moil and blows of life-contending strife may have perpetrated deeds of apparent cruelty, it becomes a veracious chronicler's duty not only to pen the glory-crowning deed of chivalry but likewise, if perpetrated, the deed that "smells to heaven." Only thus can balanced truth be properly brought into the white light of correct understanding and survey. A reviewer of historic incident should veto all personal bias, bigotry, and truth-dishonoring duplicity. If it be a sorry fact that the pains-taking reviewer clearly discovers that there exist institutions, proud and prosperous, whose historic baskets contain no small number of addled eggs, it becomes sterling honesty to place truth's label thereon. This has not always been done by knowing writers, hence, many sincere-minded people have paid a high price for such institutional commodity as has been wholly worthless. However this may be, the illustrious Order of St. John of Jerusalem, of Rhodes, and Malta, can well afford to submit to the investigator's closest inspection, today as of yesterday.

CONTENTS

Chapter		Page
I	JERUSALEM IN AFFLICTION	15
II	THE RISE AND SWAY OF MONASTIC ORDERS	30
III	THE "LOCUST" SCOURGE OF MOHAMMED	44
IV	HOW THE HOSPITALLERS OF ST. JOHN THE ALMONER BECAME THE KNIGHTS HOSPITALLERS OF ST. JOHN THE BAPTIST	63
V	THE KNIGHTS OF ST. JOHN OF JERUSALEM	91
VI	THE KNIGHTS OF ST. JOHN OF JERUSALEM IN STIRRING CONFLICTS	114
VII	THE CRUSADE OF EUROPE'S KINGS, AND THE VICTORIOUS DELIVERANCE OF ACRE	137
VIII	THE KNIGHTS OF ST. JOHN AT CYPRUS AND RHODES	170
IX	THE KNIGHTS OF THE ORDER OF ST. JOHN AS THE KNIGHTS OF MALTA	202
X	THE SIXTH LANGUE OF ENGLAND, SCOTLAND, AND IRELAND; ITS DISSOLUTION AND RESUSCITATION: AS ALSO A REVIEW OF THE ESTABLISHMENT OF THE ORDER IN AMERICA	234

ILLUSTRATIONS

	Page
SIR W. HENRY LANNIN	Frontispiece
MAP OF THE MOVEMENTS OF THE KNIGHTS HOSPITALLERS ON THE MEDITERRANEAN SEA, 1291-1798	67
GERARD, REGENT OF THE HOSPITALLERS OF ST. JOHN	70
A GROUP OF WAR WEAPONS	81
A GROUP OF SHAFTED WAR WEAPONS	87
RAYMOND DU PUIS, FIRST GRAND-MASTER OF THE KNIGHTS OF ST. JOHN	104
THE ISLAND OF CYPRUS	172
THE WALLS OF RHODES	192
DE L'ISLE ADAM, LAST GRAND-MASTER OF RHODES	198
THE HARBOR OF MALTA	210
MARSAMUSCETTO HARBOR, MALTA	215
STRADA SAN GIOVANNI, VALLETTA	221
JEAN DE LA VALETTE, GRAND-MASTER AT MALTA	224
MALTA—THE OLD CITY GATES	230
THE SCOTTISH WARRANT	249

"Truth comes to us from the past, as gold is washed down from the mountains of Sierra Nevada, in minute but precious particles, and intermixed with infinite alloy, the debris of centuries."—Bovee.

CHAPTER I

JERUSALEM IN AFFLICTION

"Lives of great men all remind us
We can make our lives sublime,
And, departing, leave behind us
Footprints on the sands of time."

THERE is both mind and spirit inspiration in familiarizing our minds with the earnest life deeds of noble-hearted men.

Intensely interesting to the student of bygone times is the remarkable and long-continued history of those brave, chivalric, and religious men who for centuries opposed the cruel power of the Crescent by the Cross of the Order of St. John of Jerusalem, of Cyprus, Rhodes, and Malta.

It was the great and godly Gentile apostle Paul who declared, "It is good to be zealously affected in a good thing." To thus become zealous, of necessity a man must equip his mind with a proper knowledge of that which constitutes the "good thing."

Confessedly, the author will bring to the reader's attention little more than the fringe of the robe of historic weaving, for as has been very nicely said: "Truth comes to us from the past, as gold is washed down from the mountains of Sierra Nevada, in minute but precious particles, and intermixed with infinite alloy, the debris of centuries."

Thus it becomes an edifying writer, who prefers to pen truth, rather than mind-beclouding legend, to carefully sieve out the gold from the mass of alloy. It has been the author's studious endeavor to do this, hence, with a proper degree of confidence he maintains the hope that the interesting facts outlined may be to the reader's mind illumination and spiritual benefit.

No city that has been upreared by the toils of men has had such a history as the city of Jerusalem. This famous city has been rebuilt from out of ruinous heaps no less than eight times. It has suffered the terrible horrors of twenty-eight sieges. Egyptians, Assyrians, Persians, Grecians, Romans, Arabians, Turkomans, and, lastly, Europeans, have each in their sword-unsheathed-turn besieged its walls, and appallingly shed blood upon its streets.

A brief word as to the city's geographical location: Located in the country of Palestine, it rests on a mountain crest some thirty-two miles inland from the Mediterranean Sea at an elevation of 2581 feet, while Jordan River eastward eighteen miles, courses more than 3000 feet lower than the city.

Nineteen hundred years before the Christian Era began, a priestly king, by name, Melchisedec, resided in a city called Salem (the City of Peace), where Jerusalem stands. While the Hebrew people were residing 400 years in Egypt, prior to the lifetime of Moses, Salem fell into the possession of the Jebusites, who were Canaanite idolators. When the Israelites entered Canaan under Joshua's leadership, though they made extensive conquest, yet they did not storm the mountain-fortressed city of Jebus. Four hundred years afterward, David, the illustrious son of Jesse, came to be king of Israel's twelve tribes. Though poet and musician, he was pre-eminently a bold and brave warrior. With his soldiery he valiantly stormed the strong fortress of Jebus, and possessed it in the name of Jehovah. David moved his royal court here, and uniting the original name Salem with Jebus, called the place *Jerusalem*.

What made Jerusalem especially known as "The Holy City," was the fact that David caused the sacred Ark of Jehovah's covenant to be deposited therein. This Ark, by Jehovah's command, was made by the Israelites while traversing the Wilderness of Arabia under the leadership of Moses. David's wise, princely son Solomon, at the dying request of his distinguished father, erected a beautiful temple to Jehovah in Jerusalem. Millenniums of years had passed from Adam's day, and yet this was the first temple built and dedicated to the worship of Jehovah.

All was peace and comfort throughout Solomon's reign. There was no enemy to conquer, nor was there need of moneyed expenditure for warlike preparation. Scripturally it is recorded of this delightful time of peace,—"And Judah and Israel dwelt safely, every man under his vine and fig tree, from Dan to Beersheba, all the days of Solomon." Righteousness exalted Jerusalem; sin brought humiliation and terrible woe.

Towards the close of Solomon's luxurious reign, he became in much a libertine. His plurality of wives, many of them heathen in belief, fatally led him astray. Ten of the twelve tribes revolted after his death, and winds of trouble blew.

Egypt's heathen king took advantage of the weakened throne of Jerusalem, entered the city with an army, and despoiled even the temple of its immense treasures. How humiliating!

Some 250 years afterward Assyria's fierce monarch with a vast army besieged Jerusalem, took it, and carried its king a captive into Babylon. Some years afterward the Egyptian king again marched against the city, and imposed a heavy tribute upon the Jews. Years passed. At last Babylon's monarch marched a great host against this mountain city. It was doomed to be destroyed by the heathen host. Its king, Zedekiah, was led in chains to Babylon, and there slain. Thousands of Jews were enslaved. This destructive conquest occurred B.C. 589. The Jews hung their harps upon the willows by the waters of Babylon's river, and wept when they remembered

Jerusalem. Babylon's great capital city falling into the grasp of the Persians toward the close of the sixth century before the Christian Era, the captive Jews were granted permission by King Cyrus to return to Palestine and rebuild Jerusalem.

This they did, and also in the course of some years re-erected the holy temple. Again were the Jews a nation, though tributary. Time rolled onward. The marvelous warriors of Macedonia, under the intrepid and skilled generalship of Alexander, surnamed "the Great," swept like a swift leopard, ravening for prey, into Asia. The unnumbered hosts of loose-living Asiatics were overpowered, and lastly, the Jews' capital was compelled to open its mighty gates to the world's conqueror.

Alexander suddenly being stricken by death, his extensive empire fell into the power of his four chief generals. The general who ruled Syria and Egypt, did not respect Jerusalem, hence, by the basest strategy he gained an entrance, stripped it of its valuables, and led many of its citizens captive into Egypt.

Again, B.C. 200, the heathen king of Syria besieged Jerusalem, possessed it, and, in the most abominable manner, polluted Jehovah's holy temple. He sacrificed swine on the sacred altar to his god, Zeus.

A noble Hebrew family of patriotic men, the

Macabees, sternly arose as the punishers of the Syrian marauder. By almost superhuman energy the brave warrior Jews delivered Jerusalem from the villain's hand of blood and debauchery.

Again for a brief period of years did a Hebrew king sit enthroned in Jerusalem.

At this epoch, Rome's iron legions were conquering the world's nations. Pompey, a famous general, was subduing, and bringing tributary to Cæsar, the Asiatic peoples. He conquered Syria, then marched into Palestine.

Jerusalem fell into his power. Pompey respected the holy temple, and left it unplundered, yet he caused to have the city walls broken. Thus in B.C. 63, Jerusalem became a tributary city to imperial Cæsar.

Herod, an Arabian, was raised by Julius Cæsar, B.C. 43, to be Procurator over Judea and Jerusalem.

He it was who thought to murder the holy child Jesus, born in the village of Bethlehem. But Herod could not accomplish the demoniacal deed.

We have swept swiftly down nineteen centuries to an amazing, divinely significant event—the birth of earth's Redeemer and Saviour, Jesus the Christ.

How closely the history of old Jerusalem was interwoven into the terrible web of earth's crimsoned conflicts!

Historically, the writer's endeavor will be to set

forth the startling fact that this sacred mountain city has throughout later centuries continued to be the war-inflicted city, and shall be to the close of the Gentile times. Yet there is predictive hope for battle-scarred Jerusalem. Let us continue our steppings on history's pathway.

The "Babe of Bethlehem" grew to manhood, and ever loved Jerusalem. Seated on Mt. Olivet, as he viewed the beautiful city of David, the Sacred Records tell us that he wept, and breaking into vocal lamentation, exclaimed, "O Jerusalem, Jerusalem, thou that killest the prophets, and stonest them which are sent unto thee, how often would I have gathered thy children together, even as a hen gathereth her chickens under her wings, and ye would not. Behold, your house is left unto you desolate."

Full of self-exalting pride and jealousies, the Jewish officials of Jerusalem arrested and had cruelly crucified the Son of God in A.D. 34.

Jerusalem had become a veritable hot-bed of seditious and political plottings. At last, rebellion ripened into bloody revolt against Cæsar's laws. Vespasian, an eminent Roman general, and Titus, his warrior son, moved their iron legions to Jerusalem's overthrow. The Jewish citizens were closely beleaguered within their strong-walled city.

Catapults and enormous battering rams were brought into play against the city's mighty walls.

On July 15th, A.D. 70, the Roman soldiery entered in merciless fury, and an appalling slaughter ensued. Historians affirm that a million Jews perished with the fall of Jerusalem. The magnificent temple, the marvel of the world, was utterly destroyed. Not a stone was left in its walls. This awful overthrow was declared by Titus to be a divine judgment, as it certainly was. How remarkable it was that the Romans destroyed it in the same month and the same day of the month, July 15, as had the Babylonians centuries before!

For years afterward it appeared as if the levelled city was doomed to time-lasting desolation. But not so. In A.D. 117, Rome's Cæsar, Adrian, conceived the plan to erect a Roman city on its stone ruins. This was done, and he named the new city, *Ælius*. But no Jew was allowed to come within certain prescribed leagues of the city for nearly 400 years.

From an ancient village of mud huts, upreared on the banks of the Italian river Tiber, Rome in the passing centuries had become, at the epoch of Jerusalem's destruction, a mighty city of surpassingly grand palaces of marble.

The ever-vanquishing legions of the Romans, under famous generals, had conquered earth's nations. Even insular Britain became tributary to the imperial Cæsars. The wild sons of Ishmael, of Arabia's deserts, alone retained their independence. Rome's treasury was thus kept full, while the empire's marine merchantmen swept the great sea, and poured abundance of food stuffs into the imperial city, supplying all citizen freedmen gratuitously. Immorality, like a hideous unclean beast, devoured citizen virtue. The very religion of the Romans was an engine to the increasing growth of prostitution and impurity of life.

From Octavius Augustus, the first crowned Cæsar, B.C. 25, there reigned no less than forty-two Cæsars in the passing of three and a half centuries. Many of the list were poisoned, some stabbed to death, others were compelled to take their own lives, like luxurious Nero. Still, there were a few Cæsars whose reigns were sagacious and virtuous. Both Vespasian and Titus, his son, were noble exceptions to the venal rule. Titus ruled as Cæsar but three years. Doing good was with him a passion. If, perchance, a day passed in which he considered he had done nothing of worth, he would sorrowfully exclaim, *"Perdidi Diem!"* (I have lost a day.) This sentiment has come down to us in the lines:

> "Count that day lost, whose low descending sun
> Views at thy hand no worthy action done."

In this emperor's first year of reign, A.D. 79, the cities of Herculaneum and Pompeii were buried beneath the ashes and lava of Vesuvius.

But time and topic forbid my dwelling on Cæsar's history. We must hasten onwards.

From the missionary days of Christ's intrepid apostles, the soul-converting truths of Christianity, in quiet power, ceaselessly filtered throughout the extensive empire of Rome. Multiplied engines and inhuman modes of torture, from century to century devised against Christ's servants, but added to the growing church of Christ. The Gentile nations had their enriched temples of marble in every city; yet what is not of truth inevitably ends in rot and ruin. This is the logic of history, in civil affairs as also in the realm of religion. The dragon of Paganism vainly fought to break the sword of holy truth in the possession of the soldiers of the Cross.

The forty-second Cæsar of Rome, Constantine the Great, professed the Christian faith in A.D. 325.

As regards Constantine's spirit and character, as also his religious status, much could be set before the reader which, in the light of historic truth, would evidence his unworthiness to be considered a Christian. For example, he promised his sister, Constantia, the wife of Licinius, to spare her husband's life, then surreptitiously caused him to be killed. He caused his eldest son, Crispus, to be banished from Rome, and then had him murdered. His own wife, Fausta, because of a rumor as to her infidelity, was inhumanly suffocated to death by the emperor's command. From the highest authority we are told "he was at best only half heathen, half Christian, who could seek to combine the worship of Christ with the worship of Apollo, having the name of the one and the figure of the other impressed on his coins." Sir Knights of Malta, at least those who are historically enlightened, do not revere the memory of Constantine, yet as an Order, professedly Christian, it recognizes the spiritual worth of the militant phrase, viz., *"In Hoc Signo Vinces."*

We are told that, the night before the decisive battle of "Milvian Bridge" was fought between the Roman legions under Constantine on the one hand and the more numerous legions of Licinius on the other, Constantine beheld in the vault of heaven a flaming red cross, and above it the gleaming words, "IN HOC SIGNO VINCES." The words in English read, "By this thou shalt conquer."

The famous Cæsar gazed in devout amazement, and resolved upon a course of action. He forthwith caused to have made a labarum, consisting of a long gilded spear, crossed at the top by a bar from which hung a square purple cloth. At the upper extremity of the spear was fixed a golden wreath, encircling the sacred monogram, formed of the first two letters of the name of Christ.

The ensuing sanguinary battle was fought, and the legions of Constantine were victorious.

Constantine, as was quite in keeping with his

Christian profession of faith, became heartily interested in those sacred places where Christ lived and where his holy life was sacrificed. He it was who caused that the Roman-built city on Mount Zion should be henceforth called by the Davidic name, Jerusalem. Much like the mythological bird of Egypt, the Phenix, which was believed to come forth out of the desert of Arabia every 500 years, fly to the sacred city of Heliopolis, and there be consumed on the altar of Egypt's gods, rising again from its ashes, young and beautiful, —thus did Jerusalem, in concrete reality, rise rejuvenated after centuries of silence and desolation out of ashes and ruin.

Helena, the aged mother of Constantine, had joyfully accepted the holy faith of Christ, and wished not to die until her eyes had gazed upon the sacred places of Christ's earthly ministry. Though weighted with years, she made the pilgrimage to Jerusalem. Tradition says she caused careful search to be made for the cross upon which Christ was crucified, and found it. This story we may well doubt, for 300 years of sword and fire had ensued. However, if credulous, relic-revering Europeans imagine that the pieces of wood and bone deposited in their religious temples have virtue in them, we care not either to protest or grumble.

When the emperor Adrian, in A.D. 117, upreared the city of Ælius, he built a temple to Rome's god,

Jupiter, on the site where had stood Jehovah's temple. Constantine caused its demolition, and erected on the site of Christ's sepulchre a church known as "The Holy Sepulchre."

In every clime, in every revolving age, men and women are governed in mind and conduct by custom. Some personage or some society has felt impelled to do something, and, lo, very soon, like a flock of sheep following a bell-wether leader, all are spirit-impelled to do the same thing. This, too, is the logic of all history. As has been declared in rhyme,—

> "Man yields to custom, as he bows to fate,
> In all things ruled—mind, body, and estate."

Thus it transpired that after the aged mother of the Cæsar pilgrimaged to Jerusalem, from every part of the great empire, especially from Europe, devout-minded Christians wished not to die without visiting as pilgrims the spot where Christ suffered for mankind's transgressions.

The clergy fully acquiesced in such a devout desire, and were ever ready to pronounce a benediction upon all who took up the pilgrim's staff, and especially upon those who, ere they departed on the arduous and perilous journey, placed to the credit of the clergy the keeping or disposition of their earthly estates. Thus it was that pilgrimaging greatly added to the increasing wealth of the Church; and in exact ratio the temporal enrichment of the Church increased the power and authority of the clergy. The leading bishops could no longer say in the words of the apostle Peter, "Silver and gold have I none."

The European peoples, deeply plunged in superstition, accepted the Empire's change of religion as a matter of political expediency. Time-serving prelates arose to fleece the sheep of Christ, not to lead them by still waters and in truth's green pastures.

Time rolled its resistless wheels onward. Julian, the nephew of Constantine, came to be Cæsar in A.D. 361. He was schooled in philosophy, and hated Christianity, that is to say, the Christianity of the times. As Cæsar he tore from the Church all temples of the old religion, and rededicated them to the gods. Christians were thrown out of all offices. Christ had declared that the Jewish temple would not only be destroyed, but its sacrificial ceremonies would come to a time-lasting close.

To contradict this, so we are told by Julian's enemies, though we may well doubt this to have been the Emperor's motive or desire, he gave orders to all Jews to begin the rebuilding of their temple in Jerusalem. Great was the rejoicing of the Jews. Prodigious preparations were begun, but when the army of laborers were removing the piles of ruins, explosive fires flamed suddenly up and drove the workmen away from the sacred spot. Julian's project utterly failed.

In a sanguinary battle with a Persian army, this apostate Cæsar was pierced by a javelin. Tearing the missile from his mortal wound, history declares him to have exclaimed,—"O Galilean, thou hast conquered!" Of course, you need not be told that it was Jesus Christ whom he meant, as Jesus had been reared in Galilee. As none but endeared friends were near the youthful Emperor's person through his brief agony, we have proper grounds for doubting his having spoken these words.

CHAPTER II

THE RISE AND SWAY OF MONASTIC ORDERS

"When the devil was sick
The devil a monk would be;
When the devil was well,
The devil a monk was he."

THE hey-day of the heavenly teachings of the unselfish Nazarene, of Jesus the Christ, compassed the years of the earth life of his disciples, the twelve Apostles, and the years of their direct successors. In other words, the first and second centuries of our Era were pre-eminently the years of truth propagation, with Spirit power accompanying the Gospel message to men. It was in those years that our Anglo-Saxon forbears became enlightened and instructed in the knowledge of divine truth. Paul of Tarsus, Luke, the physician, as also the apostle, Andrew, it is believed, preached in Britain. Julius Cæsar, the noble Roman, some years prior to his elevation to the Consulate, had led his legionaries into Britain, subjugating the tribes to the laws of the Empire of Rome. However, a numerous body of men and women openly refused to recognize the great Roman's subjugating mandate, and fled to the rocky fastnesses of what is known as Wales, thus preserving to our day many of the unique customs, as also language, of the pre-Christian Angles. Who has not heard of the fearless Caracticus, and the brave and militant Boadicea, who in storm and stress led their poorly armed warriors against the ironic might of Cæsar's legions, desperately striving to beat back the almost invincible host of trained soldiery? The soldiery of Rome never crossed the sea to make conquest in Ireland to the west, known to the Romans as *Hibernia,* the Green Isle. Alas! the unalloyed Church of the divine Master, like unto its Head, was destined to behold the uprising of men, astutely politic, indeed, yet wholly devoid of the spirit of its Founder, who in self-seeking professed and secured leadership, despoiling the fold of its precious heritage, the power and freedom of the Spirit of truth. In his writings Paul penned a prediction as to this infamy manifesting after his death. He referred to such men as "grievous wolves."

It is well for the reader to know that profound wisdom and learning was possessed by various templed schools throughout eastern nations in those times. Chaldean, Egyptian, Persian, and Grecian magi, or masters, had throughout the speeding centuries probed deeply and tirelessly to learn all cosmic laws, as also the why and wherefore of universal things. Thus gleaning many pearls of wisdom they were competent to perform amazing enactments which were miraculous to the minds of the unlearned. This knowing of Nature laws and forces was no evil, neither was it any possession of the Satan of superstition, as shallow-minded religionists have averred. Truly, ignorance of the warp and woof of the garmenting of Deity, that is, of Nature's laws, is more the product of the power of darkness than aught else under the sun. It is of moment to consider the truth of this ere the hurtling dart of condemnatory invective be thrown at those who in every way were the peers of their detractors. In this connection it comes not amiss to bring to the reader's attention ere passing that within the temples of pre-Christian centuries, which in their architectural moulding, as also furnishings, all was patterned to conform to things celestial. In them the various powers of Nature were tabulated, and typed by terrestrial forms or things which in their living nature and varied dispositions shadowed the invisible powers of superearthly realities. To the unenlightened, alas, these material replicas were things not only sacred in themselves, but to be worshipped as gods. While this was a fatal error, and as such, evil, as it led to much abominable folly and increased mental stupidity, those of to-day who choose to live in "glass houses" of ignorant thought do not increase in true wisdom by stone-throwing at the "gods" which neither they nor their forbears correctly appraised. Moreover, how unspeakably inconsistent it was in those who in solemn Councils condemned as of Satan's invention and property all which they termed, Heathenism, and to prove their zeal and detestation desecrated and despoiled all Gentile temples, and after thus doing, as time flowed onward, in very many ways brought into their own places of worship the like furnishings, as also patterned ceremonial rites which, beyond all successful contradiction, were originated and used in Gentile temples! Of course the unlettered religious masses were not enlightened so as to sense properly the inconsistency of it all, and it may have been that the introduction of the ancient religion's typical furnishments in Christian temples filled a want in the minds of the millions whose fore-parents worshiped in view of these very things.

The author has chosen to briefly touch upon this phase of truth in history so that he may the more properly set forth the root source of many things which in our times are recognized and assented to as comprehending religion's massive and polyglot tree. Verily, it is men's thoughts as to things earthly which, in the last analysis, weigh good or evil. The things possess no evil in themselves. This is philosophically true, yet erratic, impulsive, and frequently fanatic men and women act as if their imagined devil was in reality the thing they hated. The writer of this historic sketch is in no ready mind to dispute the falsity or correctness of such mental picturing. Be it remarked, however completely furnished, in an exoteric aspect, and however sense entrancing did the professed Church of the homeless Nazarene become, by its rulers thus purloining—this term is properly used—from religion's predecessors, the reader should know that the spirituality of primitive Christians emasculated their minds of all thought as to any living need of gorgeous and extravagant ceremonials. The inner light of truth, as also the demonstration of the Spirit, fully satisfied. Their God and Father was an ever-present Spirit, and their divine Teacher did not instruct them to look toward and glory in Babylon, Egypt, Greece, Judea, Arabia, or Rome, as repositories of their Father's treasury of wisdom and blessing. Not at all. They understood differently, for after their Teacher's cruel murder, Peter declared, "I perceive that God is no respector of persons, for in every nation he that feareth (reverences) him and worketh righteousness is accepted with him."

After Constantine was diademed imperial Cæsar, the better to centralize his august person in the midst of his tribute-paying nations, as also, as some historians have set forth, to remove from the luxurious city which the bedeviled Cæsars, his predecessors, had in every infamous manner besmirched, he chose to upbuild and wondrously embellish the old city of Byzantium, situated on the shores of the Bosphorus, the deep-channeled strait which separates Europe and Asia. He gave his new city his own name, Constantinople; that is, the City of Constantine. Throughout this Cæsar's reign, both the social standing, as, also, in a very sententious aspect, the policy, of the Church underwent a change. The change was material, not spiritual. The very word *spiritual* took on, as years passed, an altogether different meaning. What was its churchly meaning? Naught else than that the Christian clergy constituted in their official persons divinely delegated authority among all and over all men; that, hence, the Church in essence and action comprehended the voice of the clergy. Thus spirituality was sourced in church officials, and to be in obedient accord with ecclesiastic power was to be spiritually disposed; to be opposed thereto was judged to be heretical.

Now to those who read the pure teachings of the primitive pupils of the Christ, the term *spiritual* has an altogether different meaning. Thus, Jesus declared, "When he the Spirit of truth is come, he will guide you into all truth." The Spirit came and imbued them on the day of Pentecost in Jerusalem, not in Rome. And the beloved John wrote, "Ye need not that any man teach you for ye are all taught of God."

Alas! the millions of scattered people in Constantine's day were neither booked in the Greek or Roman languages, hence the original Greek writings of the Apostles, nor the Latin translation of the Bible by the scholar, Jerome, of the third century, could be studied by them as a sure preventive against the mind-beclouding superstitions of the times. The inward light in the personal soul was soon displaced for the external effulgence of a religion of show and discipline in accord with the demands of the Church. Still, beneath all formalisms and cold parade, however popular they be, there inheres in the religious soul a deep vein of unspoken piety as also a strong desire to experience more consciously the true spiritual power. The more worldly external religionists become, and the stronger among men the sirocco winds of sensuousness blow, the keener are the longings in many to divorce their persons therefrom. This, then, is the root reason for the existence of Monasticism among the nations. By no means was John the Baptiser the first ascetic, for such a wilderness course of living was inaugurated centuries ere his life-time. There inheres in such a mode of living something far other than, as some may think, mental delusion. The fact that many men have preferred such a mode of living evidences that in social environment there is the matter-worshiping pull which stoutly tends to insulate and stultify the hidden springs of man's soul. But, then, while monasteries, hermitages, nunneries, sodalities, divorce from worldly associations, each member carries with him, or her, his own *shade*, or if the reader prefers the term, devil. Thus it was that this world-renouncing passion led multitudes of men to dwell in isolated localities from year to year, and in the humblest manner sustain life in their bodies. These confraternities however, being recognized by the ruling classes, and lands as also varied material gifts being from time to time given them, naturally awakened in their souls the devil of cupidity, as also affected, more or less, their mode of living, and fostered indolency of behaviour. With increased largesses their membership increased, much as a highly furnished and well provisioned sanitorium of today attracts to it an increasing number of comfort-loving "patients." In the end this catering to the easy mode of life became an actual peril, a menace to social stability. When King Henry VIII of England quarrelled with the Church Pontiff, he found no less than six hundred monastic institutions in his island realm, each a drain on the work-a-day population. The stern king did not hesitate to confiscate their landed estates to his own regal disposition, and forthwith drove them from his realm. He, true to his nature, "took the bull by its horns," and despatched it. As to the justice of the ensoured monarch's conduct in the case, it is not the writer's prerogative to declare. However, if the whole truth was bared it need not be surprising to find the king to have been innoculated with the same virus as the indolent monks, that is, with greed. Still, as a monarch, had he so willed, he could the more serviceably use the great properties.

As it is of an Order, both monastic and militant, which impelled to the writing of this treatise, it will not be amiss to inform the reader that nearly 700 years prior to the founding of the Hospitallers of St. John, in 370 A.D., or thereabout, an Order was founded in Cesarea, Palestine, by St. Basil, known as the Order of St. Lazarus. It was a hospital for the housing and care of men stricken with the dread disease, leprosy. At its founding none but lepers comprised its membership. In fact a constitutional law of the Order made it impossible for any man who was not a leper to become its Grand Master. This old Order had its Lazaretts in many localities, and though we are not told it functioned in Jerusalem, yet it was famously known by all nations, and was the worthy recipient of continued gifts from far and near. True, it was in no sense a knighthood Order, until after the Hospitallers in the eleventh century became, by pontifical right and suffrage, remodelled as such, as further on it shall be shown.

After Constantine forsook Rome by establishing his throne in Constantinople about 325 A.D., naturally enough, the head bishop (patriarch) over the eastern Greek-tongued churches, at the Emperor's will, likewise made the fair city his abiding seat, and, moreover, took on greatness with the capital's growth and increasing regality. Constantine attested his sincere interest in religion by erecting what was the finest and grandest church edifice upon earth in his royal city. He gave it as name, St. Sophia, that is, the Church of Divine Wisdom.

From their humble beginnings the Eastern churches carried on their ennobling work in the Greek language, the language of culture and philosophy, while the Western churches used the Latin tongue of the Cæsars. This linguistic difference was, in a measureable degree, responsible for church dissentions and divisional antipathies between the east and west of Christendom, so called.

The old Roman capital, it is easy to believe, received a staggering blow when Cæsar moved therefrom. However, this condition did not long continue, for subsequent to Constantine's death a Cæsar gave imperial ruleship ere he died to his sons, Valentinian and Valens. To the former was given all western, that is, European, dominion, to the latter all eastern sovereignty. Shortly after this division of the vast empire of the Cæsars a hotly contested dispute arose between the two metropolitan Patriarchs of Rome and Constantinople. It appears that he of Constantine's city assumed the sounding title, "Universal Bishop." Bishop Gregory of Rome stoutly opposed the assumption, and by letter accused his proud brother Christian of pulling Antichrist's oar. The upshot of the dissention, as time winged by, was that by Cæsar's assistance Rome's bishop won out and assumed the title.

In those title-squabbling years the healthy blooded and strong armed barbarians from the forest homes of northern Europe swept southward, sternly inflexible in purpose to kill and flay the old "Wolf of the Tiber," Cæsar's Rome. Thus it transpired that in 476 A.D., the Cæsar of the West, Romulus Augustulus, was compelled to bow his head to uncrowning at the stern hand of the barbarian chieftain, Odoacer the Goth.

The clerical power of the Bishop of Rome was by no means nullified by the overturning of Cæsar's throne. By the superstitious barbarians the Bishop in his robings of glory was freely accepted as Heaven's vicegerent, and, of course, it was the astute policy of the church prelate to have them so consider him. While the claim duly placed the bishop more securely in his influential seat, giving him what went for spiritual prerogative, it undoubtedly was the Eastern Church which preserved and fostered mental culture, for after Cæsar's uncrowning there fell over Europe a pall of ignorance and mental inertness, properly termed "The Dark Ages." The scattered clergy, as also their religion's devotees, became more and more steeped in ignorance while all manner of religious rites and superstition's bric-a-brac were consecrated as part and parcel of Catholicism. A word in passing as to this term: the word is wholly Greek in composition, yet, strangely enough, it has been adopted and usurped by the Latin Church. What other is this but literary purloining?

Doubtless the reader has heard that it was in the Christian monastic institutions that the learning of by-gone centuries was wisely appraised and preserved throughout the dark barbaric centuries. This, admittedly, is a fact, and for no other cause or virtue these institutions, in this valued regard, have earned honorable recognition. Roman churchmen of today do boastfully make much of this historic fact, taking, of course, all honor to their institution, but they must know that monks, hermits, and ascetics, were a far different species of religious men, in every measurement superior men to their pompous, bauble-garnished Church rulers. Not only so, they must know that not so much in the Latin language, and its European offshoots, were the writings of the past enstored, but in the Greek language. To the Latins, at least to ninety-nine per cent of them, the Greek tongue was dead letter, as much so as the hieroglyphic writings of old Egypt. True it was that not all Latins became mildewed ignoramuses, yet the enlightenment of the tribal masses of Europe was in no way a passion of the Church officials. Enough for the laboring millions if they unquestioningly revered and obeyed as flocks their bellwether overlords. But now the reader's attention is called to such relevant matter as may be of greater interest to him.

As the old imperial city of Rome was respected, if not loved, by the peoples of earth, and its name was held as a synonym for power, ruleship, jurisprudence, and material riches, at the passing of its line of Cæsars all this appraised valuation fell into the possession of the man who professed to sit in "Peter's Chair" of spiritual prerogative. As to it being an indubitable historic fact that the apostle Peter founded the bishopric of Rome, or dwelt in Cæsar's city on the Tiber, was not the scanned question of those easy-believing times of which we write. There indeed was not a scrap of writing from Peter's hand—although he wrote two epistolary letters to the scattered Christians —to attest the very important matter that Rome was his universal seat of spiritual overseeing. On the other hand, however, there exists incontestable proof in the New Testament writings that the apostle Paul resided as a State prisoner in Rome in the reign of Nero, the luxurious pervert. In truth, Paul's penned letter to his youthful co-missionary, Timothy, plainly declares that, incarcerated as he was in Mamertine dungeon, "only Luke is with me," while his brethren, Demas and Crescens, had left him. Really, then, if Peter then dwelt in Rome as Pontiff over all church societies, how indeed could Paul remain oblivious to the fact? Moreover, in the last analysis, if Peter lived not therein as universal bishop, it surely follows that the Church of Rome's claim to the professed "Chair of Peter" is based on falsehood. Leaving this statement with the reader, it will be mind illuminating to trace in reviewment another telling historic incident ere the chapter be closed.

All historic students who have read to instruction and truth enlightenment are fully aware that after Cæsar's loss of sovereignty there mysteriously appeared in the Roman bishop's hand an official document, duly inscribed and imperially signatured, professedly by the great emperor, Constantine, in which it was set forth that the emperor decreed as a sovereign gift to Rome's bishop the Italian provinces, together with the city of Rome. This document was a forgery, yet for a thousand years it was referred to as sufficient proof of the Pope's territorial and sovereign rights. The dead and buried Constantine could not prick the bubble of falsity with the sword of truth. "The False Decretals" as a document has been proven infamous, and even Roman writers now confess it is wholly unworthy of honesty's regard. But it was the stout leverage by which the Latin Bishop gained elevation and territorial possessions. He became a sovereign lord in this manner.

CHAPTER III

THE "LOCUST" SCOURGE OF MOHAMMED

"Truth crushed to earth shall rise again:
The eternal years of God are hers;
But Error, wounded, writhes in pain,
And dies among his worshippers."

THE Cæsars of the East continued to rule in unbroken line from Constantinople after the Western throne was entombed. While tribal territories in Europe were being mosaiced into various tongued nationalities, as also England o'erswept and subjugated by the Normans, led by their redoubtable William, the Eastern Empire—popularly called "The Byzantine Empire"—was a vast polyglot of Greeks, Asiatics, Syrians, Romans, Cyprians, Jews, Egyptians, and so forth. Intermixed with these citizens were ready-handed corsairs scouring the seas, and unnumbered entented plunderers throughout the lands. As to the social status of the East, a reputable writer observes, "The Eastern Empire, though equally cursed with a succession of slothful and feeble-minded princes, continued to hold together for several centuries, supported more by the memory of its departed greatness, than by actual strength. Idle pageants and voluptuous enjoyments emasculated the imperial despots, who left their power to be usurped by venal parasites, and their frontiers to be defended by hireling swords. At the beginning of the seventh century the Euphrates was still the Asiatic boundary of the Eastern Empire, which stretched southward as far as the Arabian sands. But every province was ripe for insurrection; and when Heraclius succeeded to the diadem, he found the Persians masters of Syria and Palestine. It was at this juncture, when the Roman and the Persian were competing in mortal strife, that the wilds of Arabia sent forth one of those ambitious and mentally virile men, Mohammed, whom Providence seems to have specially appointed to scourge nations and humble kings." It is at least philosophical to hold the thought that this wonder-working descendant of Ishmael the son of Abraham by the female bond-servant, Hagar, in every earthly sense possessed as much right to dethrone self-sacrificing monarchs and secure real-estate thereby as they and their progenitors had in past time. To the writer it smacks of o'erbearing presumption to say that any man or class of men possess unimpeachable and permanent right to earthly or heavenly authority and prerogative. Strip such aristocratic men of their regal and clerical apparel, of their bediamonded crowns, rings, and showy gew-gaws and baubles, and in their nakedness we may query, in what personal way are they distinctly superior people? Both as to mental equipment and muscular development there exist myriads of men, unknown and unvalued socially, men without heritage, who are their betters. And as for Church and State, which twain has been upreared by men's hammering, chiseling, sawing, planing, and nailing, what Voice from out the eternal past has declared either the one or the other to be a part and parcel of the ever-existent universal forces? The devout-minded poet was exactly right in declaring that

"Change and decay in all around I see."

And change is often essential to purity and physical and moral health, while decay implies chemic disintegration to other cosmic uses. It is, at least, a change of mental diet to duly consider this aspect of things terrestrial. Men have ever striven to bolster up their "rights," and struggle to retain their grasped possessions, vehemently decrying as infamous the like conduct of other men who set about to accomplish that which they or their predecessors accomplished by the sword, astute diplomacy, or dishonest trafficking.

The Arabian's mind, as also his manner of living, it must be fully granted, was distinctly diverse to the minds and mode of living of those whom he and his people dethroned and destroyed. Mohammed—this word means "the Glorified"—was born 571 A.D., in the desert city of Mecca. This child, soon after his birth, was left an orphan, and was reared by Aboo-Taleeb, his uncle, who, as he grew, instructed him in the shrewd art of commerce. It is no cause for astonishment, nor for unneccessary comment, that all western writers have heaped invective and superlative obliquy upon the illustrious Arab's name and memory. Largely it was the influence of both the Latin and Greek churches which impelled to this inveterate enmity. Admittedly, from both a secular and religious point of view, this man gave the professedly Christian world a time-lasting scourging, not only while he lived in person but at least for a full century after his death. The scourge duration herein mentioned, that is, about 150 years, refers directly to the Arabian conquests, not to the aftermath of Turkoman eruptions and other Asiatic hordes of human butchers. No wonder is it that modern students who read St. John's "Apocalypse," the book, Revelation, have interpreted the seer's vision of the uprising of the swarms of destructive "locusts," with stings in their tails, as having its fulfillment in the devastating on-sweep of Arabian soldiery, under the dread banner of their intrepid Prophet and leader. A writer of no mean distinction in referring to Mohammed declares him to have been "the most crafty and most successful imposter that ever assailed the faith of Christ." Now all readers of history may admit him to have been *crafty*, but whether so in a heart evil sense is a matter of individual judgment. As to his being an imposter, that is, one who subtly imposed upon his desert people, as also upon millions of others, teachings which he knew to be false—like, for example, the False Donation of Italy to Rome's bishop—cannot be proven by any living scholar or judge. And moreover, that this famous man—or, *infamous,* if you, reader, prefer,—"assailed the faith of Christ," can be properly doubted. The question which, first of all, would have to be scripturally dealt with and answered is: What in truth essence sums up the faith of Christ? If, indeed, it be thoughtlessly granted that the huge pageantry of religious ceremonial, material crucifix worship, together with the extensive "spiritual" authority of enrobed ecclesiastics of the Church was "the faith of Christ," then beyond all dispute Mohammed did mercilessly assail all this, and, moreover, in much won his spurs of conquest. However, leave we this ground of bickering and surly contention, and proceed onward. An Arab widow, named Khadijah, possessing material riches, becoming enamoured of the beautiful youth, Mohammed, although she was older than he, chose him as her husband. He, it appears, had successfully managed one of her commercial caravans. As to what subsequently was enacted we read "Hitherto he had led a voluptuous yet not disreputable life; but, all at once, he affected to become a strict penitent, and retired to a cave in Mount Hira, a hill near Mecca, where, under the guise of great austerity, he perfected the gigantic project with which his brain was pregnant. Having brought it to maturity, he affected to make a confidant of his wife, by declaring to her, that, through the ministrations of the angel Gabriel, he had been favoured with special revelations from heaven." Now there is biographical fact herein before the reader, yet with it the coined spleen and invidious bias of the writer's mind and spirit. The prudent reader will accept the wheat of fact by sifting from it the chaff of duplicity placed to the discredit of the long dead Arab leader and law-giver. It is so easy to be a traducer of the person who "follows not us," reading into his conduct and spirit, in the most unscrupulous manner, the thoughts which are the spawn of our own breeding relative to him. This is a very vicious but altogether too common an evil under the sun, and bears the fruit of surpassing trouble. Generally, may it be said, men are not willing to "give the devil his due," but, rather, heap to his account much that is of their own enacted meanness.

And yet, the chronicler of the above statement goes on to say, "Nature, if we may credit the Arabian historians (it may be this writer disliked much to do this) had moulded Mohammed for a supreme station. His port was noble—his countenance serene and modest—his wit docile and ready—his manner courteous—his conversation complaisant and sweet. He was, moreover, liberal to profusion, endowed with keen discernment, and possessed of the kingly faculty of placing men in the situations for which their talents exactly suited them." There certainly sounds no man-demeaning note in this penned characterization. By Mohammed's most bitter critic it must be granted as of truth that the desert scion of Hagar was wondrously endowed in mind, spirit, and body to accomplish in a few years the time-lasting work which is credited to him. Neither Alexander, Hannibal, Charlemagne, nor Napoleon, has left on the pages of history any accomplishment that measures up to the work of Mohammed. No, nor does any such measurement gleam forth from the recorded biographies of the long list of men who have been incumbents in "Peter's Chair." Another point at least worthy of passing notice is this. It has been from the East, not from the West, that mankind's most illustrious founders of soul-reforming thought have come; Abraham, Zoroaster, Moses, Gutama, Pythagoras, Hermes, Plato, Homer, Jesus the Christ, Mohammed, and many other saintly masters of universal wisdom, were natives of the Orient. The precious seed sown by many of these did not harvest in material riches or clerical pride and autocracy, to themselves or others, but it blossomed and ripened to mankind's soul-emancipation from the thraldom of sordid sense passions.

In the space of twenty-three years the Prophet had brought all the tribes of Arabia into enthusiastic allegiance to his person, while his doctrines were accepted by all as God's revealed will and word. Ere passing onward in our necessary brief review of this courageous, and in every estimate, very wonderful man, it comes not amiss to say that upon issuing from the cave in Mount Hira he brought with him a very large and unique penned manuscript which he termed "The Koran." His unhesitating claim was that its contents were naught other than the inspired revealments of truth, made known by the ministry of the great archangel, Gabriel. Coming forth, Mohammed began to convince the citizens of the sacred city, his wife, Khadijah, becoming his initial convert. The primal germ expression of his teaching was, and continues to be: "God is one; Mohammed is his prophet." To Mohammed God was holy, just, almighty, ever invisible, all-wise, and all images of man's making as expressions of saints and angels were abominations, and any degree of reverence bestowed upon them was proof of a degenerate religion. No human conduct was considered so despicable to Mohammed as religious veneration bestowed upon images of men and women in churches and at shrines. Thus can the reader understand in what distinctive regard Mohammed antagonized both Latin and Greek Christianity. Is it cause for wonder that ever since his appearance he has been dubbed "The Infidel," and his religious adherents "Infidels," by both Latin and Greek churchmen?

A veritable hodge-podge of irrational yet deep-rooted superstitions made up the religious ideas of the Arab tribes at the appearing of Mohammed. Mecca was pre-eminently their sacred city, for therein stood the Caaba, built as was believed by Sheik Abraham, when he visited his bondwoman Hagar, and his son, Ishmael. As a citizen, the Prophet here voiced his teachings, but the powerful rulers were incensed at his boldness, and soon hatched a plot to take his life. The astute propagandist eluded them, and by night fled some forty miles northward to the desert city, Medina, and therein renewed his voicings. Soon his powerful magnetic personality won to him the entire citizenship, for, doubtless, the Medina people had slight reason to love the pharisaical rulers of Mecca. Mohammed's night flight from Mecca has ever been known by his millions of disciples as "The Hejira." To all Moslems it is the beginning of their era, viz. 622 A.D.

As the Koran writings are voluminous some have questioned the truth of Mohammed having written all contained therein while in the cave of Mt. Hira. However, it is now known that from prehistoric years there were established in isolated places of earth, apart from all social communities, secret brotherhoods who spent their lives in study.

Such places were known only to those few men who to the learned master, carried the marks in their persons as being by the Spirit chosen to do a destined work on earth. Mt. Horeb was one of these sacred places, and Moses, the initiate of Egypt's secret school, journeyed there, remaining some time. Mt. Carmel was another, and Elijah, the Hebrew prophet, frequently tarried there. If, then, the cave of Mount Hira was one of such places, Mohammed may have been assisted in accomplishing the work in hand. We may well opine that much of secret matters has ever remained veiled to the merely curious multitude.

At Medina we are told how that the angel brought to the Prophet a finely-tempered sword, commanding him to use it in the telling propagation of the teachings committed to him. Unhesitatingly he obeyed, and he led an armed company against his Mecca enemies. Consternation and craven fear now possessed the rulers, as they expected naught else than death-dealing redress for their plotting his life. But the Prophet's purpose was not to avenge insult and infamy, but rather to convert his Arab people. He voiced this purpose to the citizens, and the people readily embraced his teachings, and soon became zealous and life-long propagandists, to gladly die, if need be, for the new faith's extension.

Of all people of earth for whom the Prophet possessed extreme dislike, even inveterate enmity, it was the Jews and the shaven-skulled monks of the distempered Christian Church. In his military commands to his soldiers he gave strict orders never to strike down women and children, but surely slay money-grasping Jews, and never in mercy spare the lives of such indolent monks as they contacted with in their marchings. Mohammed must have had cause for the planting of implacable enmity in his soul for Jews and Latin monks. No doubt he contacted with these classes of parasitic men in his commercial journeyings in Khadijah's caravan service, and hence, being intuitively gifted, he rightly appraised the mind and spirit of these men. As in the inferior realm of creatures there exist swarms of parasitical flies, bugs, and stinging insects, so among men there live those unproductive species who subsist exclusively upon the toil and sinew of other men. These prefer that manual labors be performed by others, while they themselves live richly off the products of honest-minded and ready-handed toilers. The man of observant mind and eye becomes aware of this evil among men, and if he be in spirit more than a selfish time-server, the fact stirs him to oppose the outlived principle. And in this connection it may properly be said that any organized religion or secular institution that in any degree caters to or remains blind-eyed to such inequality and perversity in enactment deserves condemning reproof. Why should any nation of toilers sustain and persist in allowing a toil-shirking class, either under the guise of trade or religion, unrighteously to grasp the ripened fruits of honest toilers? This indeed has been the vexed question of the ages, and remains among men a problem unsolved, and a condition of living which stands seriously in need of adjustment.

The logic of all history supports the author in saying that had Mohammed been but a military genius, a leader of impassioned and infatuated men imbued with the one thought of death-dealing war and conquest, his influence among men would have terminated at his death. But this was not the case with Arabia's Prophet, for it was his religious teachings—grant them of wisdom or, on the other hand, worthless—which impelled him, as likewise his millions of co-religionists, to subjugating conquest.

Jerusalem fell into the Moslem's grasp in A.D. 637, after having been a Roman city for 567 years. There ensued no degradation of the Cæsarian city —the writer calls it Cæsar's, for it was not Jewish built as was the Jerusalem of former ages,—nor serious spoilation. By world-recognized conquest it was won by the Arabians, led by Omar, one of Mohammed's most accomplished chieftains. There was no glaring iniquity in imposing tribute upon Latin citizens, and as for sobriety of behaviour the Moslems were, in many ways, the peers of both Greeks and Latins. The Arabian "locusts" in their subjugating conquests swarmed eastward until they reached the famous Euphrates River, upon whose bank they built a splendid city, naming it Bagdad, that is, the City of Peace. This eastern city's site terminated their exploits in Asiatic territory. However, the whole of Syria, Palestine, and Egypt in northern Africa was won by their gleaming scimitars and long spears. As horsemen warriors they were unsurpassed by any people. The famous city of Alexandria in Egypt, a city of oriental culture and riches, fell into their possession. This elegant metropolis, as the reader may know, was founded by King Alexander, the illustrious Macedonian, some centuries prior to the beginning of the Christian Era. Onward the Arabians swept along the African coast-line westward, taking as they went the old city of Carthage, the renowned capital of the Carthaginians, Hamilcar and Hannibal, the inveterate and troublous antagonists of the earlier Cæsars. Still westward in conquesting zeal the warriors of the Prophet galloped, until they reached the Straits of Hercules, now known as Gibraltar. Reaching these comparatively narrow waters they crossed over into Spain (Hispaniola), and speedily overran this European peninsula, planting therein a Moorish colony of Mohammedans. They essayed to sweep northward, but were beaten back by the soldiery of the Frankish monarch, Charles, nicknamed "Martel," that is, the Hammer. Thus it was that although the Arabian conquests terminated, the filtration of Mohammed's teachings, it appears, had converted the minds of certain Asiatic tribes in Persia and other countries bordering on the Euphrates. These were Kurds in nativity, and, it is said, in past years had worshipped a sword placed upright in the ground.

Territorial possessions on earth have always, even to the present hour, been the major cause of international and tribal warrings, whether, indeed, the holders were religious or non-religious. It is truth to say that formal religion, however garnished, glorious, and worldly refined, in no degree divorces from men's minds and hearts the love and passion for real estate riches; in fact, its possession is as tinder to the flame of strife and official enmity. Thus it was that the extensive territorial possessions of the Prophet's successors became bones of contention between the two families which claimed blood lineage with Mohammed. The Arab chieftain, Ali, had married Fatima, the Prophet's favorite daughter, while Abubeker, the father of Mohammed's favorite wife, Ayesha, became his successor, that is, the Caliph. The city of Bagdad was chosen the capital city of the eastern territories, while the other caliphate ruled the extensive Egyptian and other territories from the city of Cairo. As time went by much dissention ensued between the two caliphates. The question of superiority and sovereign right was an intangible one and through the centuries has continued to be the Mohammedan bone of contention. However, let not the reader think that the Moslem problem as to rightful succession to a seat of power was or is exclusively a Mohammedan tangle, for it is a fact of history that what is called "The Chair of Peter" has been the cause of hot, hateful, and hurting jealousies, purchasings, as also acts of infamy. In sorry truth historians—and Papal historians at that—record the fact that a certain claimant of the pontifical chair who for a time sat thereon, after his death and burial was, as a lifeless corpse, robed in state and placed in a judgment seat, with a jurist to plead his case, and judgment pronounced against him as a contumacious usurper. After pronouncement against the dead, his right-hand fingers were amputated and his corpse tumbled into the Tiber. All this was inhumanly perpetrated in the name of Christ's religion! It doubtless is true that few there live today who are knowing as to such terrible deeds having been enacted, while many there are who are ready to declare such statements heinously false. To the latter class the writer of this treatise will refer them to the Papal commended volume *The Chair of Peter*, by Count Murphy, wherein the incident is recorded. It was the body of Pope Formosus upon which this inhuman act was imposed by his successor, Stephen VI. Formosus, Bishop of Porto, became Pope in 891 A.D., and died in 896. He was the 110th Bishop of Rome. The historian says of him,—"he drank no wine, that he never tasted meat, and that he died a virgin in the 80th year of his age." As to Pope Stephen we read, "Stephen was driven from the see (chair) and was thrown into a dungeon and strangled there."

Now in the annals of Mohammedanism the student will scan in vain to discover any such atrocious deed. There indeed have been infamous Caliphs, merciless to their enemies, but a like deed imposed upon an official's corpse has not been recorded.

Leaving this horrid incident of history let us pursue the course of events which led to the establishment of the order of Hospitallers of St. John of Jerusalem. It may be news to the knightly reader to be told that two centuries and a half prior to the founding of the Hospital of St. John the great and good king of the Franks, Charlemagne, caused a hospital to be built in the Holy City. As to this fact we read, "In the year 799 Jerusalem was once more in the possession of the Christians. The Caliph Harunal Raschid, admiring the talents and virtues of Charlemagne, and being willing to alleviate the sufferings of the pilgrims, presented the emperor with the keys of the Holy City. Charlemagne readily availed himself of the various privileges which resulted from this invaluable gift. A hospital and library were erected at Jerusalem, at his expense, for the use of the Christians; and he gave other proofs of his liberality, although he did not visit the Holy Land himself." It is cheering to know that this illustrious Frank was himself a scholar and appraised properly the value of the dissemination of knowledge among earth's peoples. In this, he differed from the purpose and conduct of those who sipped the juice of knowledge and gave the juiceless rind to the masses of mankind. The friendliness which existed between Charlemagne and the Mohammedan Caliph worked good-will in Palestine, for a quaint rhymist has recorded as follows:

> Christian men, both far and near,
> Long afterwarde, for many a year,
> Yeden their way to Jerusalem,
> To the Sepulchre and to Bethlem,
> And to all other pilgrimage
> Withouten harm or damage.

The reader may rightly think that the years whereof we write were stirring with ever-changing events. The Mohammedan propaganda had affected and, in a great measure, changed the thoughts of millions of men. Rome's Europe-reaching Church had gone to seed and vitrified the minds of its devotees. True, there were here and there wisdom's true sons who lived in obscurity, and who, to protect and prolong their lives while studying Nature's wondrous laws and forces, penned their discoveries in allegory and by the use of symbolic language and glyphics which to matter-minded churchmen were unfathomable. This fact is now known by those of today who possess the occult key which alone can unlock their treasury of wisdom. But as this is a theme which comes not under the purview of our minds in this treatise, we rightly forbear to dwell upon it.

The territorial jealousies, together with what has been called the spiritual authority, of the two sovereign Caliphates, Egypt and Bagdad, soon broke forth into internecine warrings. The province of Palestine was again o'erswept with armed hosts, and while these warrings were rampant the Persian Turkomans, under the famous chieftain, Togrul-beg, snatched the luxurious city of Bagdad from the Arabian Caliph. This event occurred in 1055 A.D. His son, the famous Alp Arslan, a very oriental Napoleon, gained a masterly victory over the Greeks, making a prisoner of Romanus Diogenes, the luxury-loving and loose-moralled emperor of Constantinople. Arslan's son, Malek Shah, forced the Saracens (Arabians) out of Jerusalem in 1065 A.D., and thus the Turks were in possession. Prior to this event the Hospital of St. John the Almoner was founded in Jerusalem, and its humanitarian work was being carried on most creditably under the supervising care of a noble-hearted man whose name was Gerard. The ensuing chapter will bring before the reader's mind, in as clear and concise a manner as possible, the growth and chivalric deeds achieved by the Hospitallers of St. John.

CHAPTER IV

HOW THE HOSPITALLERS OF ST. JOHN THE ALMONER BECAME THE KNIGHTS HOSPITALLERS OF ST. JOHN THE BAPTIST

"Oh, hallowed memories of the past,
Ye legends old and fair!
Still be your light upon us cast,
Your music on the air."

THREE succeeding centuries from the halcyon years of the good and wise Charlemagne, the generous Frank who, by the way, was crowned by the Pope's hand on Christmas Day, A.D. 800, with the iron Crown of the Cæsars, had brought about intolerable conditions throughout Palestine, for the Turkish rulers manifested naught else than deathly enmity towards Christian pilgrims, who, in their superfluous fanatic zeal, trampled in an unceasing stream towards the Holy Sepulchre at Jerusalem. We may consistently opine that this inveterate enmity of the Turkomans was in no sense a one-sided evil, for, be it known, the religious Latins were deeply schooled in hate for any and all religions which in word and spirit were contrary to that of Rome. It is justly proper to declare this, for it is a constitutional ingredient of the Latin Church to inveigh against and hate all other religions.

We of today may deem it to have been naught

else than a fanatic craze and impulsion—as it truly was—which caused the multitudes from European countries to hazard life and limb in such dangerous trampings eastward, but doubtless had we been living in those unbooked times, wholly under the spell of the Latin Church's claims, we would have done the same thing, and, it may be, left our carcases to regale vultures and jackals in Asia Minor or Syria. "Do as the Romans do" carries weight in the opinion of mental copyists in every age. The exceptional person is considered even today by time-servers a peculiar mortal. However, it is such peculiar people who sum up the valued weight amid the lightness and levity of humanity.

It appears that maritime merchants whose vessels trafficked between Italy and the Palestine coast ports, gleaned many a well authenticated tale of the invidious and cruel persecutions which befell the unfortunate pilgrims from the western countries from the heartless assaults of Kurdish maurauders. This fact is not surprising, for every country, east and west, was infested with merciless brigands,—in fact, brigandage was a profession—who defied both civil and religious law. Today, as of yesterday, it is not prudent to travel alone through certain European countries without an armed guard or attendant. What, then, must conditions have been in those earlier years we may clearly conjecture, when human life was accounted a small matter indeed. Then, also, to die by some sudden blow while in so sacred a pursuit to the popular mind was to secure a sure passport into the felicities of paradise. In truth, Popes declared such journeying to be a sin-absolving certainty. And what more valued pronouncement could be vouchsafed? Surely, then, unlearned pilgrims could bank on at least post-mortem blessedness if, perchance, they suddenly "shuffled off this mortal coil" while engaged in so laudable an enterprise. And as for their earthly possessions, the glorious Church would increase in material enrichment by their demise. The author will have occasion to touch on this phase of historic fact further on.

It appears that these merchants of Amalfi, in or about the year 1050 A.D., had influence with the Caliph of Cairo, Egypt, whose name was Monaster-Billah, and by giving him a very costly present gained permission to build a church in Jerusalem. This edifice was dedicated to St. Mary ad Latinos. Two hospitals were also erected, one of them dedicated to St. John the Almoner, the other to Mary Magdalene. As to the date of this building event historians differ a year or two. Both dates, 1048 and 1050, have been set down. We are credibly informed that St. John the Almoner, or the "Charitable," was neither the Evangelist not the Baptist, but a certain Cyprian (native of Cyprus) who had been Patriarch of Alexandria. In the seventh century when Jerusalem first fell into the hands of the Arabians, he sent money and provisions to the afflicted Christians, and supplied such as fled into Egypt. Subsequently when the Hospital monks became a military order, they renounced the patronage of the Almoner and placed themselves under the more august tutelage of St. John the Baptist, at which time they became known as "The Knight Hospitallers of St. John." It will be of interest to submit an authoritative statement as to the work taken in hand by the self-sacrificing men of this fraternity. "These charitable establishments were open to the suffering of every persuasion, and even the Moslems received alms. The members of the Christian church were entertained without distinction of nation or condition. There they clothed again such as had been stripped by robbers; there the sick were treated with care; and every kind of misery found, in the charity of these Hospitallers, a new kind of mercy to relieve it." In the able work of Robert Morris, LL.D., *Coins of the Grand Masters of the Order of Malta*, it is stated that it was monks of St. Benedict who served in the Hospital at its founding. Other authorities, however, state that when it was duly recognized as the order, "Hospitallers of St. John of Jerusalem," it was under the rules of St. Augustine. Be that as it may, the work faithfully performed was highly commendable, and was generously supported by those philanthropic mer-

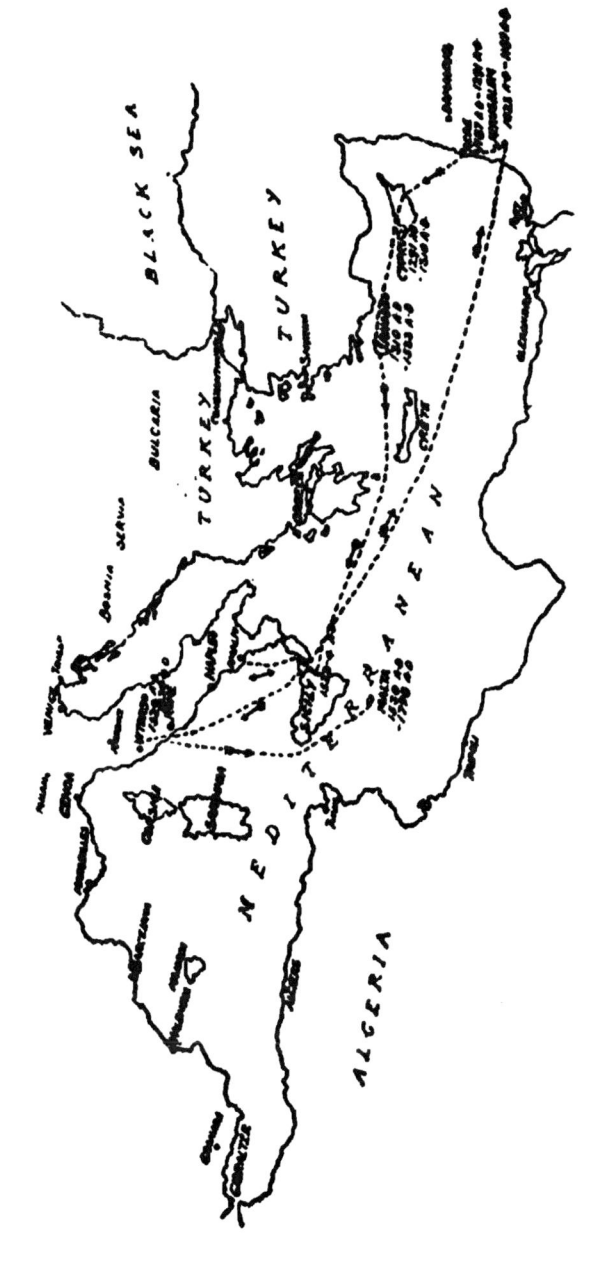

MAP OF THE MOVEMENTS OF THE KNIGHTS HOSPITALLERS ON THE
MEDITERRANEAN SEA, 1291-1798

chants who sensed its need and importance. Those who became Hospitallers took three distinctive vows, viz., Chastity, Poverty, and Obedience. Their lives were consecrated to the service, and there is recorded no desertion or apostacy of their number.

It appears that a native of Provence, France, by name Gerard Tunc, joined the monks of the Hospital shortly after it was built, and he being a prudent and purely virtuous man, was chosen by the serving brothers as Rector, that is, Overseer. The monks wore a regular habit, consisting of a plain black robe, upon which, on the side next the heart, was attached an eight-pointed cross of white linen. In the preceding chapter the author recounted the overthrow of the Arabian rule in Jerusalem and Palestine by the Turkomans, who, although they had espoused Mohammed's teaching, did in no degree stay their lust to grasp territory from the Arabians, and glean riches by plunder. Then, also, as they were subjects of the caliphate of Bagdad, and the Palestine Moslems were of Cairo, Egypt, they possessed little if any secular regard for those whom they supplanted. In much this unfraternal status of the two Mohammedan houses had its counterpart in Christendom between the Latin and Greek citizens of the two contentious capital cities. Scarcely seven years had elapsed from the Hospital's founding when the blood-spilling Turkomans took Jerusalem as their prey. Now there was increased need for Gerard and his serving brethren. Handicapped though they were in many trying ways, they persisted in their Christian labors.

Though the European nations were soon apprised of Jerusalem's adverse change in rulers, the fact of knowing appeared not to daunt the courage or change the purpose of men to pilgrimage to the Holy City. The writer in this connection proffers the remark that nothing conspires to make men so bent and persistent in will and act as deep-rooted religious belief, whether the belief is senseless superstition, or, on the other hand, inspired truth.

Historically considered, there was a cause for increasing pilgrimage in those truly dangerous years which few readers of today are enlightened upon. It was as follows. A certain hermit of Thuringia in Germany, Bernhard by name, had preached that at the end of a thousand years from A.D. 1 the fetters of Satan would be broken, and the earth would be consumed by fire. Moreover, ere the fiery deluge, Christ would appear on Mount Zion at Jerusalem and gather the Christians to himself. This belief took possession of multitudes, and swept throughout the western nations. Beyond doubt, it imbued many with the pilgrimage craze, and the clergy were not slow in using it to Church enrichment in earthly posses-

GERARD, REGENT OF THE HOSPITALLERS OF ST. JOHN

sions. Of truth, they never have been sensitively modest in this material regard.

It is the exact truth that very many pilgrims were unmercifully, yes, inhumanly treated at the hands of robbers and assassins, while the ruling Kurd in Jerusalem remained heartlessly indifferent, so long as tribute money flowed into his sordid hands.

Pope Gregory VII, spurred to act by the Greek Emperor, raised an army of fifty thousand men, promising to lead them in person to Jerusalem and overthrow the infidel oppressor of his people. Alas! the Pope was no sort of a Moses, for not like unto that illustrious man he did not choose to suffer the afflictions of his people in camp life, so that neither he or his army started eastward. Later, when this Pope had gone the silent way of all the earth, it was uncouth and unkempt Peter—a genuine Peter who had no pompous chair—a French hermit, that had the honor of being the stirring instrument who caused all Europe to awaken to Jerusalem's distress and affliction. The Hermit had made the pilgrimage, and being an exceptionally shrewd man, he succeeded in getting both to and from Jerusalem alive and well. With a letter of appeal for urgent aid from the Patriarch of Jerusalem, he journeyed to Rome to bestir, if possible, the Pope to action. Pope Urban listened to the sturdy hermit recount his personal experience, also facts which he had gleaned from other sufferers. Then the Pope read the Patriarch's stirring appeal, after which he gave the Hermit authority to voice a crusade in the name of the Church. As to the person of Peter we are told, "He was a little low hard-favoured fellow, and therefore, in show, more to be condemned than feared; yet under such simple and homely feature lay unregarded a most subtile, sharp, and piercing wit, fraught with discretion and sound judgment, still applying to some use what he had in his long and painful travel most curiously observed. The oppressions and profanations that were his theme,—his long uncouth beard—his naked feet—his extreme abstinence—and his austere and holy life, won for him the reverence of a saint, and the fame of a prophet; and prince and peasant alike burned with pious impatience to hasten to the East, and deliver Palestine from the unbelieving race."

In a strictly worldly sense this crusade, awakening to the ridding Palestine of another people than the Jews, can be consistently viewed, but in the white light of New Testament teaching, the pure doctrines and spirit of the Master of men, it focalizes as a huge and glaring anachronism, a direct contradiction of Christian teaching. But assuredly it was religious, as fully and sincerely so as was the earlier uprising of the Arabian converts of Mohammed. It may be truly declared that man-welded and assembled religions, diluted as they ever are, more or less, with superstitious imaginings, invariably implant hate and unfraternal oppositions in men's souls, and always are strife producing agencies among men; whereas the pure and heavenly teachings which powerfully tend to veto all partiality, the lust for power and earthly honors out of men's souls, actuate to peace, fellowship, and good-will to mankind.

As in the Roman Pilate's day in old Jerusalem the soldiery of Cæsar used the cross to destroy victims of their displeasure and condemning, even thus, after the lapse of centuries, the Latin Church used the cross—the same emblem—to spur Europe's soldiery on to destroy its enemies. Here, then, the writer pens a thought which the reader will do well to consider carefully. The divine Teacher did not preach strife or retaliation for ignoble injury. When his disciple would use the sword, his quiet command was, "Put up thy sword in its sheath." But the Master's doctrine has never been practised, in any full laudable manner, by the Latin Church, however strenuously it has vaunted the claim to full and exclusive right in the possession of Christian authority.

Pope Urban summoned a council at Plancentia, at which, we are told, four thousand of the clergy and thirty thousand of the laity were in attendance. At this initial council definite crusading seed was sown, but its effective blossoming was effected at a little later council, held at Clermont,

France. At this later council Urban was both vociferous in stirring appeal, and, withal, very ingenious in statement. With other words the historian informs us that "he explained the supineness of the Greeks, and the necessity that existed for interference on the part of the nations of the west; observing, with great naiveté, that those who lived in the east were under the influence of a scorching sun, and had, therefore, little blood to spare; and that it behooved those who lived in a different climate, their blood flowing luxuriantly in their veins, to shed it freely for the sake of Christ. To those joining the Crusade he promised plenary forgiveness of sin and heavenly beatitude after death." This pontifical ebullition stirred the vast assembly, as a sudden and strong autumn wind stirs the tinted leaves of a forest, and one thought and emotion found vehement expression. The words, "Deus vult! Deus vult!" (God wills it), were shouted by one and all of the multitude. Afterwards these words were used as the crusaders' battle-cry.

Pope Urban of course was aware that he voiced a physiological fib in referring slightingly to Oriental lack of blood. He was astutely politic enough to apprehend that a crusade movement in no degree would financially impoverish the Pope's exchecquer, but no doubt would increase the same. As an old writer remarks, "The Popes were the only gainers by the great adventure; and all other princes of Europe, when they cast up their audit, found themselves losers." However, this historian completely overlooked the post-mortal gain to the tens of thousands, who, though losing earthly riches and their lives, had for pay the Pope's promise of sin-forgiveness and heavenly beatitude, whatever the latter words may have meant. As recorded proof that the "Chair of Peter" profited by this hot-headed movement, the following submitted fact from an authoritative pen is our attestation. "Eustice, the brother of Godfrey de Bouillon, sold all his possessions to the Church; and the other leaders of the crusade acted in a similar manner, their example imitated by persons of every rank in society." There, reader, you have it in black and white. Just how and from where the Latin Church—that is, of course, the ruling clerics—came into possession of the wherewithal, the metallic pabulum, to negotiate successfully such wholesale buyings,—well, the close-observing student of our present times need not have occasion to ask such a question. The Latin clergy have ever heaped to themselves fame as being earth's most successful money-getters. This fact impelled the pen of an olden time rhymster to write:

> In olden times, so I've been told,
> The crosier was wood while the bishop was gold;
> But now 'tis most clear without being told,
> The bishop is wood while his crosier is gold.

None of the monarchs of Europe took up the crusader's sword in this first crusading movement. It will be interesting, doubtless, to the reader to learn the names of the sturdy and chivalric leaders who led eastward the mighty host of religion's warriors. "Of the princes who acted as leaders in the first Crusade the following were the most illustrious; Godfrey de Bouillon; his brothers, Eustice and Baldwin; Robert Curthose, Duke of Normandy (brother of the King of England); Stephen, Earl of Albermale; Roger de Clinton, Bishop of Lichfield; Odo, Bishop of Bayeux and Earl of Kent; Robert, Count of Flanders; Stephen, Count of Chartres; Adhelm, Bishop of Puy, (the Pope's Legate); Raymond, Count of Thoulouse; William, Bishop of Orange; Hugh, Count of Vermandois; Bohemund, the son of Robert Guscard; and his cousin, Tancred."

We may in all truth remark, the crusade enthusiasm was unspeakably intense throughout all Europe. High and low were alike infected. Such is a law of human life. The science of psychology reveals to us the fact that strongly impelled thought, magnetically imbued, is amazingly infective, for good or ill. Its subtle power grips minds as in a vice, and it takes a strong will to free the mind therefrom. If, then, it be toned with religion, and accepted as the will of God, the reader need not be told as to the grip it possesses.

The illiterate masses of men, being peculiarly

addicted to religious influence, and also, no doubt, smelling personal license and lawless liberty in crusading trampings abroad, urged the Hermit to be their leader to Jerusalem and to start forthwith. Peter, it appears, yielded to their crazy demands, and choosing a certain soldier of fortune whom he knew, Walter Sensavier, known as "Walter the Penniless," as captain over some sixty-thousand undisciplined and, in much, conscienceless freebooters, he started on the fateful wild-goose chase.

This fanatic mob upon reaching Bulgaria found their food at low ebb, and without parley overran all villages and towns, robbing and murdering the surprised citizens. At last the natives armed themselves and in reprisal slaughtered hundreds of them. Upon the filthy swarm reaching the suburbs of Constantinople, the Emperor Alexius, being astutely politic, summoned the two leaders into his presence, and submitted to them his magnanimous (?) plan to ship them across the Bosphorus into Asia Minor, the territory of the Sultan of Nice, which famous city was his capital. The Emperor informed them that by report he had learned that the Turkish army was at a distance, hence if the crusaders would move forward at once they could without much opposition enter Nice and enrich themselves at the Sultan's expense. The Emperor's shrewd proposition was most greedily assented to, and as speedily as possible they were shipped out of his dominions. It appears, however, that the wise Hermit concluded that it would be safer for him to return westward, and await the moving of the war-disciplined troops, hence the irrational host was forsaken by Peter. Walter, their captain, moved them toward their coveted prize, when suddenly as they journeyed they found themselves ringed completely by mounted spearsmen, a great army of cruel Turkomans. Now the Turkish *atabal* war-cry rang forth, and the horsemen closed in upon the fated and fear-stricken multitude. It is sufficient to say that hardly a man of the European mob of would-be crusaders escaped with his life. After the slaughter ceased, the Sultan commanded that the tens of thousands of corpses be piled into an enormous pyramid, and left as a fear-inspiring witness of Turkish judgment inflicted upon those who chose to antagonize his sovereign prerogative.

It will not be improper to tarry at this point of our historic survey and query: In the last analysis who, if any among men, merited responsibility for this wholesale slaughter? Was it Alexius, the Hermit, or Urban? Which of these three men voiced initial authority to crusade to Jerusalem? The writer chooses to have the reader answer satisfactorily for himself.

The various crusade armies, under their intrepid chieftains, from various points of Europe converged in their marching on Constantinople as the point of crossing into Asia. While the Greek Emperor greeted the princes with smiling unction, he at the same time feared for his sovereignty, and after some serious eventuations, they came to mutual agreement as to a course of action. A writer informs us that "it was with secret dismay, rather than joy, that he (the Emperor) beheld this restless torrent of French, English, German, and Italian warriors, roll from the westward on his startled capital." Certainly, the pillaging of the Hermit's unkempt mob must have weighed upon his sensitive and furtive mind. The crusade armies, numerically, have been set down as follows. "The knights and their martial attendants alone amounted to a hundred thousand fighting men, and the pilgrims able to bear arms, to about six hundred thousand. The knights and their squires were mounted on richly caparisoned horses, and completely sheathed in gleaming steel. The former were further armed with an iron mace, a long lance, and a sword and buckler; and each independent chieftain was known by his banner." The crusaders crossed the Bosphorus and marched on Nice. They passed and beheld the horrible pyramid of European corpses, and this view set their jaws with determination to avenge the slaughter. Nice they found strongly fortified and warrior-armed. After some weeks of incessant assailing in which their loss of men was as great as their enemy, they appealed to the Emperor to have ships moved across the land to Lake Ascanius, which was near the city, and by which the citizens could secure food supplies. This was done, and after five weeks the citizens swung open the gates to the crusaders. Of course, the Emperor Alexius claimed Nice as belonging to his sovereignty, and this was agreed to after very costly presents were given to the chieftains. From Nice they marched onward, fighting as they marched, for Turkish warriors were around and about them. At last they reached Dorylaum, a very large and stoutly fortressed city. They encompassed it with a ring of steel, while all sorts of crude but powerful battering-rams were used against the formidable walls. Here they were compelled to fight one of their most bloody and notable conflicts. In the midst of the days of their incessant fightings, when many of their men were manifesting signs of home-sickness, even of despair, a report spread that there had been found the Roman spear which had been used to pierce the quivering body of Jesus on Calvary's cross. This report wondrously revived the Cross warriors. We are not told, of course, who gained possession of such a sacred relic,—perhaps, however, one of the bishops—or by what sure way it could be vouched for as genuine, neither are we told who of men had preserved it through ten centuries. However, in some conditions in life, and in certain trying times, credul-

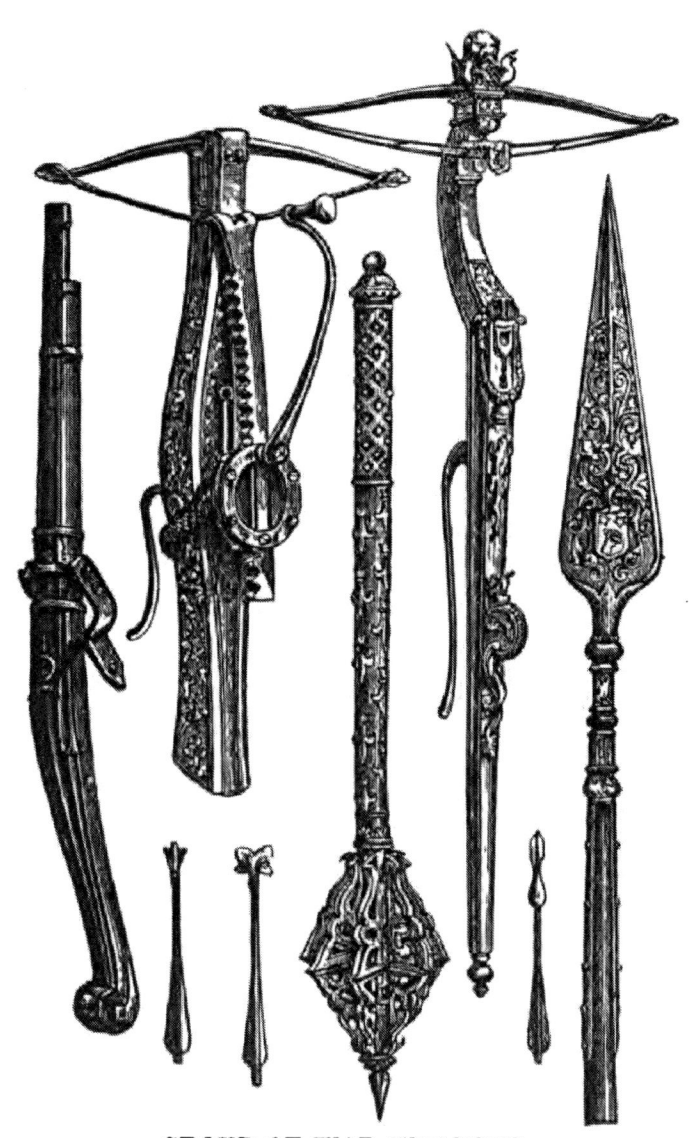

GROUP OF WAR WEAPONS
Early Musket; Lever Cross-bow; Mace;
Decorated Cross-bow; Decorated Pike; Cross-bow Bolts

ity, let it be remarked, may work to good advantage and to strengthening of purpose. Be this as it may, the reputed sacred spear in the Latin crusader's midst enheartened all, and thus assisted to victorious achievement. Four thousand crusaders were slain at Dorylaum, while three thousand Turkish captains are said to have perished. When victory was won the crusade army rested and fed to repletion. It was the army of Bohemund which took Dorylaum, while the other chieftains' armies were assailing and taking other city fortresses.

After sufficiently resting and recouping this division marched toward the opulent and great city of Antioch in Syria, northward of Palestine. The reader who has familiarized his mind with the contents of the New Testament book of *The Acts*, will know that it was in Antioch that believers in Christ were nicknamed "Christians." After seven months' besiegement of Antioch, by a price paid to an influential citizen, Bohemund and his army gained ingress. This citizen traitor caused the city's double-walled gates to be swung open one very dark and cloudy night.

Gaining entrance, after seven months of deathly struggle, the crusaders gave themselves over to rest and much surfeiting. Here they tarried for seven months in which many, weary of warring and forgetful of their initial religious zeal, returned to Europe. Careless as to food consumption, and also no doubt of sanitation, they ran out of eatables and experienced the sharp tooth of famine, and with it a death-dealing plague. As to this it is chronicled, "In the course of a few months the former (the pestilence) swept off above one hundred thousand men; while the latter (the famine) reduced the miserable survivors to feed on offal and carrion, and even on human flesh. . . . Had not the chiefs and spiritual lords, who accompanied the crusade, resorted to pious frauds to keep the host together, the conquest of Antioch would, in all probability, have been its last triumph."

In May, 1099, the fortunate survivors of plague and famine quitted Antioch, and skirting the coasts of Syria and Palestine they reached Jaffa, anciently known as Joppa. In their marching they were plenteously supplied with food by the citizens, and also by provision ships from Italian ports. Other divisions of the crusade army had stormed and taken other cities, while the brother of Bouillon had, against the wishes of other chieftains, marched to the Euphrates and grasped for himself a huge territory. This act tones to our minds the truth that territorial conquest and earthly riches played no minor part in the moving tragic drama rung into action by Pope Urban. In this connection there is a point of honor, as well as historic interest, worthy of the reader's notice. The Turkomans who had torn Palestine from the Arabian Caliphate had, it appears, crossed scimitars among themselves, one chieftain warring against another. Prior to the European crusade avalanche the Arabian Caliph had sent an army into Palestine, and regained sovereignty.

This Caliph, as the reader knows, prior to the seven years of Turkoman misrule, had treated the Christians with consideration. When the crusade army reached Palestine this Caliph was in control of Jerusalem. Dwelling in Egypt he dispatched his Vizier to Jerusalem to formulate a league of continued peace with the Europeans. Note what the historian chronicles as to the matter. "He was willing to enter into a league with the crusaders for the utter expulsion of the Tartarian spoliators; but neither his politics or his religion permitted him to accord them a permanent settlement in the land. The Christians, condemning what they held to be a breach of faith, and reckless whether their swords drank Turkish or Saracen blood, rejected the proposed treaty with disdain; and sent him for answer, that with the same keys with which they had opened the gates of Nice, Tarsus, Antioch, and Edessa, they would open Jerusalem." The reader should remember that Jerusalem had not been a Latin possession, neither a Greek, for nearly five hundred years, and also its upbuilding in 117 A.D. was the work of a pagan Cæsar. Justly viewed, the Saracen Caliph possessed sovereignty right to the city. Not only so, but the old Jerusalem of the Jews viciously cast without its gates the divine Christ, he whom these Europeans professed to adore. Of a truth "consistency is a jewel" not always possessed by self-securing men. The above may to the thoughtful reader be altogether a new angle of mind-visualizing, but the writer deems it worthy of setting forth.

Jerusalem was garrisoned by forty thousand regular troops of the Caliph, commanded by Istaker, a famous general. Besides these, some twenty thousand inhabitants took up arms for defence. The Saracen leader imprisoned within the city all Latins, and Gerard, the Rector of St. John's Hospital, was one of these. On the seventh of June, 1099, the crusade army camped before the city, and its besiegement was on. Of the seven hundred thousand fighting men who had begun the crusade march, only about twenty-two thousand were mustered at Jerusalem's besiegement. Tens of thousands were fleshless skeletons on arid battle-fields; other thousands were plague-consuming corpses around Antioch; while tens of thousands had deserted crusading toils and tarnished their religious reputation thereby. However, many troops had been left stationed in the various conquered cities of Syria and Asia Minor. As it would improperly lengthen this chapter if the writer dwelt upon, even in a measurable degree, the doings within the terrible weeks that

GROUP OF SHAFTED WAR WEAPONS
Military Flails; Marteaux; Axes; Fauchards; Corsesques;
Military Forks; Halberds; Partisans; Guisarmes

ensued ere Jerusalem fell into the crusaders' hands, the vicious struggle will be passed over. Upon the fifteenth day of July, at the hour of three in the afternoon, "the standard of the Cross waved in triumph on the walls; and, after four hundred and sixty years of bondage the Holy City passed from under the Mohammedan yoke." A recorded incident as to the kindly doings of the Rector of the Hospital while the crusaders were beneath the beleaguered city's walls is interesting. We are told that "during its (the siege's) continuance, Gerard, the superintendent of the hospital, is said to have been discovered by the infidels throwing bread to the Christians. He was seized, and taken before their general; but when the supposed bread was exposed to view, it had been miraculously turned to stone. Gerard was dismissed and permitted to continue his former practice, and the stones which he threw from the city walls at the besiegers were converted into bread. Thus the Master of the Hospitallers was in favor with both parties." The average reader may smile with incredulity upon reading this recorded performance, but to many people, then as now, such marvelous enactments in no way strain their powers of belief. These take all such stories as unquestionable fact, and moreover would consider the doubting person one to be religiously discountenanced, even under condemnation's ban.

The crusaders, when they rushed into Jerusalem, lost all sense of mercy and human sympathy. It is authoritatively declared that "all who showed the smallest disposition to resist were hewn down; and, for three whole days, promiscuous massacre and pillage prevailed. Ten thousand miserable beings, who had been promised quarter, were barbarously put to the sword; and infants even were butchered in the cradle, and at their mother's breast. In the court of the Mosque of Omar, a structure built on the site of the famous Temple of Solomon, to which thousands of fugitives fled as a sanctuary, the Latin knights rode fetlock-deep in Saracen gore." Now there had ensued no such hellish butchery as this of the Christians by their antagonists when the Arabians under Omar in 637 A.D. took possession. Does not the fact attest that the Mohammedan was more imbued with the spirit of Him who died on a Roman cross, than those Europeans who religiously, at least, revered the cross?

CHAPTER V

THE KNIGHTS OF ST. JOHN OF JERUSALEM

"With the eye of a spirit I look on that shore,
Where pilgrim and prophet have lingered before;
With the glide of a spirit I traverse the sod
Made bright by the steps of the angels of God."

OF all the crusading chieftains, Godfrey de Bouillon was the most famed for piety, considerate conduct, and chivalrous spirit. In every way he was a true and noble-hearted leader of men. Religiously, to him, the Latin Church comprehended in earthly power and movement the complete zodiac of divine religion. Now it is quite easy to sense this belief of very many people, for the reason that they view the external organization as the institution which the Christ founded among men, when the truth is that he founded no external institution other than having with him for three and a half years twelve men who were his students, that is, disciples, and who became apostles, in other words, mission-sent proclaimers and demonstrators of his divine doctrines.

If the writer mind-visualizes the primitive records aright, those gospelers among men, throughout their lives, did not uprear any external edifice and declare it to be the Church, but rather to them the Spirit-led believers constituted the

Ecclesia, that is, the Christian Assembly. True, the primitive believers were fraternally united, and in assembling together performed, as occasion required, the rites of baptism, as also the partaking of bread.

It is justly proper to appraise any and all existent institutions, not by the judgment of those men who are influential rulers in and over them, and who are sustained by them, but, rather, by the moral and mental effects which they outwork in the lives and conduct of those who make up their membership. "By their fruits ye shall know them," declared the Master, and he in this uttered a truism. All organizations change, not only in outward appearance, but, what is more vital, frequently in spirit. So it was with the Hospital of St. John in Jerusalem. At its founding there was no thought as to military action or relationship. Its exclusive work was humane and philanthropic. In this it was truly Christian. Not only so, but its labors were wholly apart from all religious bias and favoritism. What it took upon itself later, is now the interesting matter which will be brought to the reader's attention.

When Jerusalem fell into the possession of the crusaders, a council of the leaders was held to elect a king and institute a government. To the minds of all the Europeans, what they considered a Christian kingdom was the prime factor to bring about.

It appears that Godfrey de Bouillon was properly considered the prince among princes who, in every way, was fitted to fill and do honor to such an exalted seat. Just why the Pope who chose to be held among men as Christ's earthly vice-regent did not now look upon the "Holy City" as the proper place from whence to sway the nations, and move his court therein, no reason is given, hence we can only conjecture. Possibly the tenure of peaceful possession was, to his mind, too precarious to seriously consider such a movement. Be the truth what it may, the Pope did not deem it a laudable or necessary thing to so much as visit the land in which Jesus dwelt. Godfrey was chosen and acclaimed King of Jerusalem, yet when the Patriarch was in the act of placing upon his head a jeweled crown, Godfrey interposed a refusal to wear such a symbol of exaltation. Said he, "I cannot consent to wear a crown of gold, where the Saviour of mankind wore a crown of thorns." Those were unselfishly spoken words, and reverberate down the passing centuries as attestation of this man's true nobility of soul. It will be of interest to the reader to note the recorded question which the council asked an answer to, as also the reply, as to the fitness of Godfrey. "What faults have you observed in the Duke of Lorraine?" "The only fault we find with our master," answered the voters, "is, that when matins are over, he will stay so long in church to learn the name of every image and picture, that dinner is often spoiled by his long tarrying." "Ah," said the council, "as this man's worst vice appears to us a great virtue, Jerusalem could not have a better sovereign." One of Godfrey's first official acts was to visit the St. John Hospital. He found it pressed full of diseased and war-wounded men, both Christians and Infidels. To the reader the writer deems it proper to say that in his use of the words "Christian" and "Infidel" as distinguishing names, he does so in a historical, he may say, in a national sense, for, in truth, in much the Moslem religionists manifested in conduct—and this, after all, is what counts—as great a measure of soul nobility as their enemies. Directly after visiting the Hospital, Godfrey resolved upon enriching the Christian institution by personally deeding to it the extensive landed estate of Montboire in Brabant, France, with all its dependencies. This philanthropic act of Godfrey, the "Defender of the Holy Tomb," initiated a prolonged custom of charitable givings which while laudable and acceptable worked not always to Hospitaller humility and unselfishness. Every justly good thing, we may say, must guard against the ever present demoralizing tendency. It is not the goodly action which essences evil: it is the self-enriching spirit of those men who reap and control the benefits of the virtuous-minded benefactors. It appears that Godfrey was not alone in his estimate of the St. John's Hospital, for when Raymond du Puis, Dudon de Comps, and Gastus of Berdiez beheld the self-sacrificing labors of Gerard and his brethren, these nobles forsook all thought of returning to their western homes, and voluntarily dedicated their lives to the Hospital work. Gerard now felt that the Hospital should become a recognized and officially declared brotherhood. This was effected, and Pope Paschal the Second confirmed it as "The Hospitallers of St. John the Baptist," exempting the Order from all tithes, with the privilege of electing its own superior, and wholly independent of clerical interposition. It is needless to say that this confirming act of the Pope greatly pleased both Gerard and his Hospitallers, and they had every reason to prize their freedom from clerical intrusion, and any possible pushing of power. This Papal recognition transpired in 1113 A.D.

When Godfrey was elected "Defender of the Holy Sepulchre," an honored title of his own choosing, July 23, 1099, his brother Baldwin, who had possessed himself of Edessa in Mesopotamia, journeyed thither with his retainers, while the gallant-warrior chieftain Bohemond, together with his army, returned to Antioch in Syria. Possibly it was true that the majority of the living crusaders, after Jerusalem was possessed, returned to their far distant homes. Reiterated reports as to the Christian virtues of the unselfish monks of St. John's Hospital were voiced everywhere, and such ready advertising reaped largesses to the enlarged upkeep, as also propertied influence, of the Order. Then, also, in no small degree, the knowledge that the Pope had generously recognized it and given it his blessing greatly conspired to its international popularity. As to this we may in common parlance say, "its fortune was made." A writer in touching this beneficiary phase of the Hospital remarks, "The rapid enrichment of the Hospital exalted the piety, and perhaps the pride, of the Rector; and, in accordance with the spirit of the times, he manifested his zeal by the erection of a superb church, situated on the spot which tradition pointed out as the retreat of Zacharias, the father of John the Baptist, to whom the structure was dedicated."

Godfrey did not have at his command other than a small company of retainers against any possible attempt on the part of Egypt's Caliph to retake Jerusalem. The historian Gibbon informs us that "the new king embraced his departing companions, and could retain only with the gallant Tancred three hundred knights and two thousand foot soldiers for the defence of Palestine." Surely, such a depletion did not bespeak crusade prudence, or, indeed, any genuine love for the welfare of Jerusalem.

Doubtless the reader may not be clear in mind as to the mention of knights of St. John or knights of the Temple, for neither of these orders of knighthood was at that hour in existence. Whence, then, came they? The historian Gibbon, peer of historians, will enlighten the reader as to this query. He writes, "Between the age of Charlemagne and that of the crusades, a revolution had taken place among the Spaniards, the Normans, and the French, which was gradually extended to the rest of Europe. The service of the infantry was degraded to the plebians (peasants); the cavalry formed the strength of the armies, and the honorable name of *miles*, or soldier, was confined to the gentlemen who served on horseback, and were invested with the character of knighthood. The dukes and counts, who had usurped the rights of sovereignty, divided the provinces among their faithful barons; barons distributed among their vassals the fiefs or beneficies of their jurisdiction; and these military tenants, the peers of each other and their lord, composed the noble or equestrian order, which disdained to conceive the peasant or burgher of the same species with themselves. The dignity of their birth was preserved by pure and equal alliances; their sons alone, who could produce four quarters or lines of ancestry, without spot or reproach, might legally pretend to the honor of knighthood; but a valiant plebian was sometimes enriched and ennobled by the sword, and became the father of a new race. A single knight could impart according to his judgment, the character which he received; and the warlike sovereigns of Europe derived more glory from this personal distinction than from the lustre of their diadem. This ceremony, of which some traces may be found in Tacitus, was in its origin simple and profane (secular); the candidate, after some previous trial, was invested with the sword and spurs; and his cheek or shoulder was touched with a slight blow, as an emblem of the last affront which it was lawful for him to endure ... As the champion of God and the ladies (I blush to unite such discordant names), he devoted himself to speak the truth; to maintain the right; to protect the distressed; to practice *courtesy*, a virtue less familiar to the ancients; to pursue the infidels; to despise the allurements of ease and safety; and to vindicate in every perilous adventure the honor of his character." The knowledge which the above writing gives to the reader is proper excuse for its appearance in this chapter of our treatise.

We thus learn that military knighthood antedated the founding of the semi-militant orders of which that of St. John of Jerusalem was the first. The religious orders patterned in much after the strictly military, in that in their ceremonial investiture they gave a spiritual tone to every movement in the performance. Of a fact, in those times there was no important, attractive, and usable ingredient or thing among men which the

Church did not take and engraft as a part and parcel of her furniture and ceremonialism. This policy was, in an earthly aspect, astute, yet he who reads to spiritual profit the apostolic writings cannot but discern the distinct apostacy, a complete demarcation from the Gospel economy. Of course, charitable liberality of judgment is a virtue to possess, but when it is compounded with the ingredients ignorance and indifference, the mixture is morally and mentally a fatal poison.

Godfrey must have keenly felt the quick departure of so many of his crusade companions, yet there were many vitally important matters, both of church and state, to fully engage his mind and spirit. One of the things which caused him not a little vexation was the demand upon him by the newly chosen Patriarch of Jerusalem. It appears that a certain bishop, Daimbert, archbishop of Pisa, Italy, was chosen to rule the Church in Palestine. This cleric bearded Godfrey with the demand that Jerusalem and the sea-port Jaffa should be the possession of the Church, and as the king was a loyal son of the Church this matter would forthwith be attended to. Godfrey did not assent to this cleric's demand in full, but consented to apportion one quarter of Jerusalem and Jaffa as the property of the Church. Now this important fact in history has been passed by in silence by almost all writers of crusade history, but Gibbon, who in life was free from clerical fear or carefulness as to ecclesiastical displeasure, has seen fit to enlighten his readers as to this property-grasping incident. However, this old-time claim-demanding incident stands not in isolation on history's page. The like spirit, in many ways, exists at the present hour, and is potentially operative among men. And, doubtless, there are leaders in secular affairs who are quite ready to palliate the disturbing and vexing spirits by unjustifiable acts of liberality.

Hardly two full weeks passed by from the hour of Godfrey's chosen ruleship when news reached him that a Moslem army was on the march from Egypt towards Jerusalem. It appears that when this force of warriors left Egypt, the news of Jerusalem's change of rulers had not reached the Caliph, hence the force sent was meant to strengthen the defence against the besieging crusaders by harassing their encampments. This army was under the command of Emir Afhal, a renowned warrior Saracen. He had vowed in the presence of the Caliph to annihilate the Europeans. But his impulsive vow came to naught. Military strategy appealed to Godfrey as the necessary line of action, so instead of awaiting the onslaught of this reported enemy, the Christian warriors by quick marchings southward, came suddenly in sight of the Moslems encamped on the plains of Ascalon. The city, or fortress, of Ascalon was a possession of the Caliph's. It appears that large herds of cattle were driven in the van of the Moslem army, presumably for army food. The Christian knights with their squires and staunch retainers received the blessing of the Church, and also looked upon the true Cross which the bishop caused to be raised in their midst, and thus being imbued with crusade fervor they galloped furiously towards their enemy. The animal herds first beheld them in their sun-lit mail, and became crazed with fear, and stampeded the Emir's camp. The Moslems could see but murkily for clouds of dust, while the war-cry, *"Deus Vult! Deus Vult!"* of the onrushing, intrepid crusaders threw their enemy into a fear-inspired panic. The Emir was defeated from the beginning, ere sword clashed with scimitar. He fled to Ascalon, while many of his troops were hewn to pieces. Few of the crusaders were slain, and they returned to Jerusalem heavily laden with the spoils of war. The writer of this treatise is impressed with the thought that it was because of this battle with the enemy at Ascalon, so quickly after Jerusalem's deliverance, that the new-recruited Hospitaller, Raymond du Puis, together with his brother Hospitallers who as crusade princes were skilled in arms, conceived the thought to convert the Hospitallers into a semi-military knighthood order.

What was this proud Emir's humiliation and undoing, was to the glorification and strengthening of the kingdom of Jerusalem. Gerard's order received all wounded warriors, while new and greatly enlarged edifices were upreared. Not only so, but as the order was continually receiving manorial estates and monies, in and from European countries, Gerard conceived the plan to found like hospitals in various maritime cities of the west. This was done, the better to hold, as also oversee, the estates of the Hospitaller order. These we are told were the first commanderies of the Order of St. John. These were the "houses of St. Giles in Provence, Tarento in Apulia, Messina in Sicily, and latterly Seville in Andalusia, Spain." It appears that Godfrey sent his intrepid warrior, Tancred, with his bold retainers into Galilee to take the city of Tiberius, a city mentioned in the Gospels. This city with others was speedily possessed, and in the bloom of subjugating victory Tancred marched into Syria towards the old and wealthy city of Damascus. He, however, soon learned that he lacked sufficient troops to cope with the Sultan of Syria's army, hence he sent word to Godfrey as to his army's plight and distress. Godfrey responded to the call, and beat back the encircling enemy, thus rescuing the brave and bold crusaders. Homeward they journeyed, and the Emir of Ceserea came out in peace to meet Jerusalem's king, and presented to Godfrey an offering of the country's fruits. As to the issue of the presentation, we read, "Godfrey by way of courtesy accepted a cedar apple. He had scarcely eaten this, however, when he suddenly became sick, and his knights in alarm conveyed him to Joppa. At Joppa Godfrey grew worse; and on the 18th of July, 1100, after committing the kingdom of Jerusalem to the companions of his victories, he breathed his last." The sudden death of Godfrey fell upon all Christian dwellers in and around Jerusalem like a pall of darkness, as he was loved and respected by all. His unselfish zeal was ever manifest, and this virtue was not then, as it is not in our day, a common commodity which men in official positions possess. This nobleman was devoutly laid to rest in the Church of the Holy Sepulchre.

Directly after the burial ceremony, the Barons who were in Jerusalem, together with the Patriarch, met in council to make choice of a prince to fill the royal seat of sovereignty. Much contention prevailed, for the Patriarch declared the city was the Church's possession, hence his choice alone was lawful. This wordy usurpation was in no way conceded by the princes, so the upshot of the contention was that the audacious cleric sent a messenger to Antioch to ask Bohemund to come at once to Jerusalem to take ruleship as king in the name of the Church. The Barons, on the other hand, sent a messenger to Baldwin, Godfrey's brother in Edessa, to hasten to Jerusalem to assume kingly honors. Alas for the plan of the autocratic Patriarch! It appears that unfortunate Bohemund was at the time a war prisoner in the hands of the Sultan, he having been too venturesome in his ambitious conquests. Baldwin at the head of fourteen hundred stalwart retainers came speedily to the Holy City, and upon his arrival all the citizens and soldiers heartily welcomed the warrior prince, proclaiming him as their lawful monarch. However, ere he could be crowned, the opposition of the officious Patriarch, whose hand should place the crown upon his head, must perforce be overcome. For a time the Patriarch was obdurate, but at last he yielded, and Baldwin became King of Jerusalem by secular and spiritual right. In reading the above historic fact, the thoughtful reader can clearly see how exalted rulers of the Church have mixed into, in fact, in much, initiated the contentions and troubles which men of State affairs have been called to experience. In declaring this the writer does so in the consciousness that unimpeachable historic records attest his statement to be of truth.

Return we now to the important incidents and enactments which made the Hospitallers of St. John a most illustrious and service-rendering semi-military institution, known among the nations as "The Order of Knights Hospitallers of St. John." Almost at the same time that Godfrey came to an untimely end, the Regent of the Hos-

RAYMOND DU PUI, FIRST GRAND-MASTER OF THE
KNIGHTS OF ST. JOHN

pital, Gerard, passed away. He, however, fell like a sheaf of grain fully ripe.

There ensued no discussion at his death as to who among the Hospitallers was most worthily fitted to be Gerard's successor, for Raymond du Puis was the acceptable choice of all. This illustrious man did not, as many smaller men do, work to seat himself in a larger chair than his person could properly fill, but the vacant seat demanded of Raymond that he should seat himself therein for toilsome service. The duties of Regent were no longer local, but far-reaching, and in every way trying, for hospitals of the Order were being founded in European countries, while increasing properties were coming into its possession. As Raymond and other Brothers of the Order had proved their metal as brave-hearted crusade warriors, and as the newly established Christian kingdom of Palestine was girt about with implacable enemies, it certainly was a statesmanlike thought in Raymond to utilize to the limit the militant strength of the Hospitallers for the security and permanency of the Kingdom of Palestine. Being himself a man of noble blood, doubtless he had been ceremoniously dubbed Knight, in a military way, hence as such he had vowed to use the sword upon those who presumed to o'erstep the recognized law of right, as all such knights saw the right. He, moreover, could rightly perform the knighthood action upon such men as he deemed "duly and truly prepared, worthy, and well qualified." Thus it was that he, upon taking in hand the manifold duties of the order, zealously set about the task of the order's reconstruction. First of all he brought his plan to the attention of the Patriarch, and gained the official churchman's ready assent thereto. A council was forthwith held, and, as we are told, "fresh laws were drawn up, and the brethren took an oath to defend the Holy Sepulchre, and to wage a war of extermination against the infidels. Pope Boniface confirmed the rules of the Order, and gave permission to the members to assume the title of "Knights Hospitallers of St. John of Jerusalem." In this connection, the author deems it of instruction to the reader to pen the important fact that in the year following Godfrey's, as also Gerard's death, that is, in this same year in which the Hospitallers became a knightly order, 1119 A.D., a new semi-military order was officially instituted in Jerusalem, known in history as the Knights of the Temple. C. G. Addison, in his history of *The Knight Templars*, sets the date of the founding of this illustrious Order as 1113 A.D. However, the following is worthy of particular notice. Addison writes, "At first, we are told, they had no church, and no particular place of abode, but in the year of our Lord 1118, nineteen years after the conquest of Jerusalem by the Crusaders, they had rendered such good and acceptable ser-

MALTA KNIGHTHOOD

vice (it may be as *military* knights?) to the Christians, that Baldwin II, King of Jerusalem, the cousin of King Godfrey, granted them a place of habitation within the sacred inclosure of the Temple on Mount Moriah." Now there appears in this statement a discrepancy, not only of date, but also of King Baldwin's relationship to Godfrey. Godfrey died in 1118, and as the learned author of *Military Religious Orders*, F. C. Woodhouse, M.A., remarks, "It was during the reign of Baldwin II, King of Jerusalem, that Gerard, the father and veritable founder of the Order of Hospitallers, died." Now as Gerard passed away in the same year as Godfrey, and as Godfrey's brother Baldwin became King of Jerusalem, reigning eighteen years, he it was who granted to Hugh de Payens and his eight French knight crusaders, the privilege to establish themselves near the site whereon had stood Solomon's Temple. This occurred in 1118, seven years subsequent to Addison's founding date. An old historian declares as follows, "This Order (the Templars) was founded in 1119, and took its name from the knights dwelling in part of the temple at Jerusalem." It may be quite possible that the temple this old writer had in mind was the Mosque of Omar, the Arabian prince, or Sheik, which stood where had stood the temple of Solomon. Now 1119 was the year in which the Hospitallers became a knighthood order, after a course of years' service, clearly and definitely chronicled, first as Hospital Serving Brothers, followed by the name, Hospitallers of St. John. Major Whitworth Porter in his exhaustive and erudite history, *History of the Knights of Malta*, writes as follows, "It appears distinctly enough, that the founder of the Order of the Temple did not commence the regular establishment of his small fraternity (nine French Sir Knights) till the year 1118; and the institution of that Order was not formed on a regular basis until at least ten years after that date. If, therefore, it can be proved that Raymond succeeded to the government of the Hospital on the death of Gerard in 1118, and at once proceeded to organize his brotherhood upon a martial basis, the Order of St. John claims by right the priority of formation . . . Upon a careful review of the evidence adduced on all sides, it appears that 1119 must have been about the date at which the system was inaugurated." With Major Porter's words, we will let this point as to priority rest, and move forward. However, as every sailing vessel that sails the sea is frequently compelled to tack ship, in other words, to veer from straightline coursing, the better to make head-way against opposing winds, in like manner, of enlightening necessity, the writer is compelled frequently to introduce and with brevity dwell upon matters, factors, and correlative movements which, for at least the time being, may be considered by the reader as non-essential, yet nevertheless go to the possessing of well-rounded knowledge. This, then, is the writer's reason for inserting the above in the coursing of this chapter. And, moreover, as the history of these two religio-militant Orders bears abundant witness to their indomitable doings in mutual battling against their common foeman, this treatise would be wholly out of poise, we may say, unwarrantably biased, if its author ignored the chivalrous co-labors of the Knights of the Temple. Truly, no enlightened writer who attempts to portray on printed page the amazing exploits of the Knights Hospitallers of St. John of Jerusalem, of Cyprus, Rhodes, and Malta, need entertain any pause-producing fear that the Order's heroic, self-sacrificing deeds performed can suffer an eclipsing by the recounted deeds of any other institution of brave men.

After the Order of Hospitallers was by Raymond reconstituted a knightly order, we learn that "the knights wore a black robe having a white linen cross of eight points fastened on the left side; and took (as from the beginning) the vows of chastity, obedience, and poverty. They afterwards had a red military cloak, but this was not used in the house." Of course, when they were aface the Infidel in death-dealing strife their bodies were encased in mail, as also, in a measurable degree, their horses.

In the performance of knighthood ceremonial

the action, as also utterances, were both solemn, mind-engaging, and intensely interesting. There was not the shadow, not a bubble, of that which is today termed "horse-play" manifest in conduct. The atmosphere of religion pervaded and gave breath to the refined ceremony. To life-lastingly impress the postulant with the seriousness and ennoblement of knighthood was ever in the foreground. Briefly enumerated, the following initiatory movements of investiture are interesting and illuminating.

"1st. A sword was given the novice, in order to show him that he must be valiant.

2nd. A cross hilt, as his valour must defend religion.

3rd. He was struck three times over the shoulder with the sword, to teach him to patiently suffer for Christ.

4th. He had to wipe the sword, as his life must be undefiled.

5th. Gilt spurs were put on, because he was to spurn wealth at his heels.

6th. He took a taper in his hand, as it was his duty to enlighten others by his exemplary conduct.

7th. He had to go and hear mass."

As to such ceremonial movements being original, in other words, the formulated initiatory of Raymond or his knights, we are historically assured that such was not the case. Long prior to the founding of these religio-militant orders, as has been previously touched upon, militant knighthood was a very popular factor among the ruling houses of Europe, hence we may confidently conclude that many, if not all, the ceremonial movements as above enumerated, together with others, were clearly an adaptation of the military code of knighthood investiture. True enough, the symbolic meaning, the exemplification of the action, was a mere elaborate spiritulization, although the military ritual was expressedly religious. The reader would be clearly in error in thinking that all the members of the Order were recognized postulants for knighthood honors. Such was not the case. Only those who could prove that the strain of Europe's princely families, or houses, was in their blood were eligible for knightly honors. In this aspect, the reader can understand, the Order was a close corporation, in much an institutional aristocracy. This phase of these orders was wholly unchristian in precept and policy, but in those terribly illiterate times when human savagery and barbarism as restless, turbid waters laved the walls of cities from without, the reason for, and recognition of, such a law of favoritism can be appraised more intelligently. In this connection it comes not amiss to say: the term *villain*, as used today as expressive of a basely wicked person, in the times of which we write stood for a member of the lowest order of persons, a feudal serf, a propertyless boor, and not expressive of any special moral status of the man. Our word *village* comes from the same Latin root source as does the word villain. Villagers were those simple people who dwelt apart from the wealth and vanity of cities, and anciently were completely subject to the lords and barons who heavily tithed all the fruits of their work-horse labors. This social inequality is very distinctly suggested in Shakespeare's incomparable dramas. Thus the prince of Denmark, Hamlet, declares to his friend Horatio, "By the lord, Horatio, these three years I have taken note of it; the age has grown so picked (affected), that the toe of the peasant comes so near the heel of the courtier, he galls his kibe (chilblain)." We of today may rejoice in the fact that the French Revolution in much removed the plebeian yoke from off the common people of honorable toil. However, the reader must not think that the famous Order of St. John was despotic, or toned with unprincipled ingredient. Strictly speaking, it was signally impartial in its administration, and officially degreed its membership in a wise and worthy way, as the writer will now set forth. There were three serviceable grades, or classes, of its membership. "First, the Knights, who should bear arms and form a military body for service in the field against the enemies of Christ (the Church) in general, and of the kingdom of Jerusalem in particular.

These were to be of necessity men of noble or gentle blood.

"Secondly, the Clergy or Chaplains, who were required to carry on the services in the churches of the Order, to visit the sick in the hospitals, and to follow the Knights to the field, and undertake ministration to the wounded.

"Thirdly, the Serving Brethren, who were not required to be men of rank, and who acted as esquires to the Knights, and assisted in the care of the hospitals.

"All persons of these three classes were considered alike members of the Order, and took the usual three monastic vows, and wore the armorial bearings of the Order, and enjoyed its rights and privileges."

A word of historic information relative to the recognized and official colors of both the Orders of St. John and Templars will be instructive. We find it stated that it was Pope Alexander IV, who reigned as Pope from 1254 A.D. to 1261, who decreed that the Knights of St. John should be distinguished "by a white cross on a red ground," while the Knights of the Temple should be distinguished "by a red cross on a white ground."

The reader can readily perceive how that the Pope, "in days of old when knights were bold," exercised full and all-comprehending prerogative. However, few of them lived and died happily.

CHAPTER VI

THE KNIGHTS OF ST. JOHN OF JERUSALEM IN STIRRING CONFLICTS

"The Knights are dust;
  Their swords are rust;
  Their souls are with the saints, we trust."

AS regards the definite date that the Order of Hospitallers became a recognized order of knighthood, the year 1119 A.D. has been given as historically accurate. The only value which attached to the date of the Order being reconstructed into a knighthood institution,—at least, what was for centuries deemed of special value,—was that of priority. The author does no violence to truth or the unbiased spirit of fraternity in saying that from the founding of the Order of the Knights of the Temple its members chose to manifest in many ways a spirit of superiority, hence, to concede the priority of the Order of St. John was to them irritating. Now in thus saying, it would not comport with historic truth to affirm that the St. John Knights were immune from this trouble-breeding microbe, this ungracious spirit which roots in the soul's soil. This spirit manifests in the individual, in family, as well as in institutions, religious or secular. Its influence is often felt where it is not openly shown. It is no plant in the pure Christian soil, but is a pricking weed of selfish origin and growth. Obviously enough, the robe of humility, however ceremonially symbolized, cannot be investitured on any man by another. Neither King or Pope can do this. Voiced words by no means can change the leopard's spots, or the Ethiopian's skin, for "as a man thinketh in his heart, so is he."

In the preceding chapter the reader was informed as to some important points in the making of a Knight. Before moving forward in our survey of the valorous deeds and conquests of the Knights of St. John, it will be instructive to the reader to have before him an old and accredited statement as to ancient procedure in Knight creating. From a work on Heraldry, printed in London in 1784, we subjoin the following: "The most ancient manner of conferring Knighthood was by putting the military belt loose over the shoulder, or girding it close about the waist. The first Christian Kings, at giving their belt, kissed the new Knight on the left cheek, saying, 'In honor of the Father, and the Son, and the Holy Ghost, I make you a Knight.' The first account that we have of Ceremonies in making a Knight in England was in the year 506, in the following manner; viz., a stage was erected, in some cathedral, or spacious place near it, to which the gentleman was conducted to receive the honor of Knighthood. Being seated on a chair decorated with green silk, it was demanded of him if he were of a good constitution, and able to undergo the fatigue required in a soldier; also were he a man of good morals, and what credible witnesses he could produce to affirm the same. Then the Bishop or chief Prelate of the Church, administered the following oath: 'Sir you that desire to receive the order of Knighthood, swear before God, and this holy book, that you will not fight against his Majesty, that now bestoweth the order of Knighthood upon you. You shall also swear, to maintain and defend all Ladies, Gentlewomen, Widows and Orphans; and you shall shun no adventure of your person in any war wherein you shall happen to be.' The oath being taken, two Lords led him to the King, who drew his sword, and laid it upon his head, saying, 'God and St. George (or what other Saint the King pleased to name) make thee a good Knight;' after which, seven Ladies dressed in white came and girt a sword on his side, and four Knights put on his spurs. These ceremonies being over, the Queen took him by the right hand, and a Duchess by the left, and led him to a rich seat, placed on an ascent, where they seated him, the King sitting on his right hand, and the Queen on his left. Then the Lords and Ladies also sat down upon other seats, three descents under the King; and being all thus seated, they were entertained with a delicate collation; and so the ceremony ended." In connection with this ancient record of Knight making and investing, the following old ballad is subjoined,—

> " 'Bear thou this blow,' said the King to the Knight,
>   'But never bear blow again;
> For thy sword is to keep thine honour white,
> And thine honour must keep thy good sword bright,
>   And both must be free from stain.'
>
> The monarch he lifted a Damascene blade
>   O'er the kneeling Count's brow on high;
> A blow on his shoulder full gently he laid,
> And by that little action a Knight he is made,
>   Baptized into Chivalry."

Such was the manner of Knighting a novice five centuries prior to the days of the Crusades, and, let it be known, in the author's researches of far earlier times, centuries prior to A.D. 1, much like ceremonies were enacted at the elevation of the neophyte initiate who had passed through the seven years of arduous testings of the templed Mysteries of Egypt and Greece. The later ceremonies were, in much, a revision, concision, and reconstruction of the earlier enactments, introduced into Church and State. Ere leaving this interesting phase it will not be amiss to say that what is known as the ceremonial *accolade* sums the official action of Knight designation. The word is from the Latin, *accoler*, embrace, and *collum*, neck, hence its meaning is, "The salutation given to one upon whom knighthood has been conferred, formerly an embrace or kiss, afterward a light blow with the sword."

It would be an unpardonable offence for any informed writer on Knighthood, especially so of one who has received the accolade, to remain silent as to the assistant institutional labors of the "Dames of St. John." When the Amalfi merchants gained the privilege to erect edifices in Jerusalem for charitable purposes, we read that "a chapel was built near the holy sepulchre, and dedicated to the Virgin, under the title of St. Mary ad Latinos, and at the same time two hospitals, or houses of reception for pilgrims of both sexes, were erected in the same quarter, and placed under the protection of St. John the Almoner and St. Mary Magdalene." The historian, William Waller, in this connection states, "In addition to the knights, there were Nun Hospitallers, who had a separate establishment in Jerusalem. The dress worn by these seems to have been somewhat similar in all the countries in which the order existed; these nuns were introduced into England at the same period as the knights, and they were subject to, although they afterwards acted quite independently of them. Very few particulars have been preserved respecting these female establishments; but it may be presumed they were but few in number, as Henry the Second, in 1180, ordered the whole of the sisters to be collected together, and then gave them the preceptory of

Buckland in Somersetshire for a place of residence, where they remained until the dissolution of the religious houses in 1540." It is declared as authentic that some of these Dames Hospitallers of Palestine were at times impelled to mount chargers, and, with real Amazonian bravery and zeal, exchange sword blows with the onrushing cavalry of the Infidel. Having this fact in mind, a quaint old-time English writer penned the following:

> "March on, for the shrill trumpet and the fife
> Your tongues will serve; and to secure your life
> You need no weapon,—every face and eye
> Carrieth sufficient artillery."

Now the only criticism the author of this treatise would pen as to the fatal effect of such "artillery," would be its similar results upon Christian and Infidel. Obviously, history attests the truth of our criticism. However this may be, it is indubitably true that women have in every age outlived more virtuous deeds than men. It is the mothers of the race who have and do, even prenatally, impress psychic gifts in their offspring; and such gifts, in the light of philosophy, are what tells in matured life.

With the penning of the above brief statement as to the praiseworthy Dames of St. John, we revert to the incessant strivings for mastery, as also for territorial holdings, by both Christian and Infidel. It will be of historic worth for the reader to know that while religious antagonism ever lay at the root of blood-shedding warriors, such was not the exclusive reason for much of the merciless and destructive conflicts which raged long and loud. Western princes beheld in the affluent and expansive East luscious plums of real-estate, awaiting grasping and garnering by the instrumental use of spears and swords. Having, therefore, little at home to occupy their adventuresome-loving minds, and disdaining, most generally, to spend time in any literary way, even so much as to acquire what they considered "the monkish acquirement of writing," they took up crusading as a means to a very worldly end, while the risk of forfeiting their lives in the strain and stress of martial conflict was to them a stirring ingredient. It was not so much spiritual as worldly ambition which was the spur in those tempestuous times. Had it been otherwise, the crusade leaders would have been willing to confine their territorial emancipating to the land of Palestine, and left the cities and stretches of Asia and Egypt to their long-settled citizens. But this they disdained to do. The warrior prince, Bohemund, possessed himself of Antioch in Syria as an initial prophecy of property-grasping on a gigantic scale, and with this queen city the rich province fell into his grasp. Prince Baldwin had swept eastward, as we have seen, into Mesopotamia, and stormed and taken Edessa, the capital of that province or principality. These were held as sovereignties by the princes. Thus real-estate grasping woefully weakened crusader strength, and the Holy City was bereft of trained soldiery to properly withstand all possible besiegement. Moreover, had the Europeans as to their religious profession been more consistent in conduct, in other words, had the separation of Christian and Infidel been an exclusive factor, as it was with the Knights of St. John, there would not have been bred what was looked upon as a new race or species of people in whose veins ran Christian and Infidel blood. These people were known as the Pullani, children of Syrian mothers and European fathers. In much, it was the territorial ambition of the leading crusade princes which was the selfish factor for prolonged and destructive contests of strength between the Europeans and the Asiatics. The Cross and the Crescent, of course, were inspiriting heraldic ensigns, or banners, but apart from this the moral and spiritual distinction was not so marked as an unread person imagines.

It appears that King Baldwin of Jerusalem was the father of two daughters, Millicent and Alice. The younger, Alice, was given as wife to Bohemund II, the son of the renowned warrior, Bohemund of Antioch. After this union, it transpired that the famous Count of Anjou of France, Fulk by name, pilgrimaged to Jerusalem, having, it is said by some writers, become distracted by grief over the death of his wife, by others, to show penitence for a wicked deed perpetrated. Reaching the Holy Sepulchre he, we are told, "caused his body to be scourged with broom twigs, which grew in great plenty there. Thus it was he ever after took the name of Plantagenet, or Broomstalk, which was continued by his noble posterity." King Baldwin saw in the Count a nobleman well fitted to be the husband of Mellicent, although he was some sixty years of age, and the King proposed the union, stipulating to bestow upon him as his son-in-law at his own death the sovereignty of Jerusalem and Palestine. The Count agreed to the proposal, and, forthwith, married the princess; Alice never forgave her father for thus ignoring her princely husband as to any possible hope to Jerusalem's sovereignty. Count Fulk had left in Europe his youthful son, Geoffrey, as Count of Anjou and Main. King Henry I of England beheld in this titled youth a fitting mate for his widowed daughter, Maud, his only child, hence he proposed the union and Geoffrey readily assented. The offspring of this marriage, the son Henry, became King Henry II of England, and his house, as also himself, chose "a sprig of broom in their bonnets" in memory of their grandparent having been as a pilgrim penitent stoutly thrashed therewith. Whether this broom-wearing gave rise to the wearing of what is familiarly known as the cockade to designate the wearer's partizanship, the writer cannot say. Perhaps not, for custom, as to most everything, antedates authentic history. The Plantagenet house ruled over 300 years the Kingdom of England. The famous warrior monarch, Richard Cœur de Lion, was the great-grandson of Fulk, the "Broom-Stalk," who succeeded Baldwin as King of Jerusalem. This bit of biographical history the writer subjoins as an interesting item.

King Baldwin received news that his son-in-law, Bohemund of Antioch, had been entrapped by the wily Infidel and slain in battle. The news startled Baldwin, for Alice and her infant daughter were in imminent danger, and, not only so, the King had fixed his mind on assuming the regency of that rich principality. True, there were many battles to be fought ere Palestine would be a possession, but with Baldwin "a bird in the hand was worth two in the bush," hence the territory of Palestine, with its sea-port cities of Tyre, Sidon, Acre, and others, could remain for the time being possessed by the Infidel. As the Jerusalem membership of the Order of St. John had increased amazingly, and aspirants for knighthood honors were flowing east from all princely and baronial homes, Baldwin had a large body of Knights of St. John, as also a goodly number of well-mailed and horsed Knights of the Temple, to brave the spears and scimitars of their inveterate foemen. They marched with rapidity, and unexpectedly struck the Emir's army. As to the issue we are told, "The Knights of St. John gathered their first laurels in this engagement. Baldwin, with the ardor of a redoubted soldier, flung himself into the thickest of the fight, followed by Du Puis (Raymond) and his hospitallers, and the bravest of the Christian Lords." After victory was won Baldwin and his distinguished Knights returned to Jerusalem, yet not to grow indolent by inaction, or impoverish the principality by monetary rewards bestowed. The winds of war continued to blow, if not from one quarter, then from another. If it was not the cross warriors who were tirelessly galloping towards some Moslem city or fortress, it was the soldiery of the crescent who were in their war-saddles intent upon destruction and plunder. In 1122 the Prince of Edessa, who was an impotent, happy-go-lucky chieftain, a kinsman of Baldwin, was waylaid and made prisoner by the Moslem Emir, Balak. Hearing the report, the Knights at once mounted their chargers and were off eastward toward the Euphrates with avengement in mind and heart. Of course, the wily Emir was expectantly on the lookout for the coming of his foe. King Baldwin, it appears, chose a knightly escort and in person attempted to do some scouting. Alas, he was outclassed in subtlety and was suddenly surrounded, his brave escort cut to pieces, and he himself made a prisoner of war. His main army now was set upon by a far superior host of fresh and rested cavalry, and though the Knights hewed their way into the center of the Moslem host, they at last, a remnant body, were compelled to enter the gates of Edessa to endure there besiegement with their warrior King in captivity. The reader may be sure there followed no delay when the sorry news reached Jerusalem. All alike were possessed with the one thought of deliverance and avengement. In all these death-dealing conflicts the Knights of St. John, as likewise the Knights of the Temple, were in arms the strength and stay of the Christian forces. As the Master of the Knight Hospitallers is not mentioned by historians as being in Jerusalem at this time of stress, we are led to believe that he was with his harassed Knights in Edessa. Eustace Garnier, constable of Palestine, an old warrior, with seven thousand troops and the Jerusalem Knights, marched upon the exultant foe, and the issue was a complete victory for the Christians, and the liberation of the two princely rulers. Returning in triumph to Jerusalem, ladened with the spoils of war, it was not to indulge long in rest and quietude. The Caliph of Egypt had heard of Baldwin's defeat at Edessa, and had sent an army to strike for Jerusalem's retaking. Now Baldwin upon reaching Jerusalem heard as to the intent and marching of the Infidel army, and plans were devised to circumvent the enemy. The city and fortress of Ascalon on the eastern coast of the Mediterranean, twelve miles north of Gaza, was an important possession of the Caliph. It was a storage city for army furnishment. Baldwin determined to possess this gateway for Egyptian troops. All were fully aware of the struggle which would ensue. However, this fact was no ground for doubt or cringing fear, for Ascalon must be won to the Cross. A valiant and determined army of mailed horsemen swept southward. On their march they met a small army of Moslems, and those who were not slaughtered, fled swiftly to Ascalon, pursued by the valorous and implacable Knights. Both Orders fought side by side in these encounters, and both alike were imbued with the same spirit. The Grand Masters of both the Orders led their Knights at this memorable siege of Ascalon. Just here it will not be amiss to say that this sounding title was first applied to the Regent of the Hospitallers under the administration of Hugh de Revel, who was Raymond de Puis' successor in 1267. Up to his time the name, Master, had been sufficient. It is undeniably true that high-sounding designations are not, in every instance, attestation of high class ability or virtuous behaviour in the persons who wear them officially. King David of old Israel knew this, for he wrote, "I have seen the wicked in great power, and spread himself like a green bay tree, yet he passed away, and, lo, he was not." The siege of Ascalon consumed months of toil, stress, and struggle. The strong walls remained intact, while hundreds of warrior lives were sacrificed. At last King Baldwin entered into an agreement with the Admiral of the Venetian fleet to attack both Ascalon and the merchant city of Tyre from the sea in conjunction with land attack. This was done, and after five months these renowned cities fell into the possession of the Christians. From the records we learn that the Knights of the Temple built a great movable tower with a gang-bridge on its top which could be pushed on to the top of the wall. This was moved near to the wall, but the Moslems threw down piles of wood and fired the same with Greek Fire. Oil, also, was abundantly poured on the pile. The purpose was to destroy the tower, but the wind blew the flames against the wall throughout the night. When morning dawned the stones were broken and crumbled by the intense heat, and it was no difficult matter for the Templars to press a passage into the city. Having so done, the Moslems, for the time being, were stricken with fear and fled apart from the swords of the Templars. Alas! the glaring selfishness and vain ambition of the Grand Master of this Order snatched victory away from the Christian army. With sword in hand he refused to allow other warriors than Templars to enter. The Knights of

St. John were amazed at such an act of unfraternal audacity and pride, and loudly voiced their abhorrence of such o'erbearing meanness. Baldwin was fiercely angry, yet could do nothing to change the Templar's will. At last the Moslem warriors rallied, and with shoutings pressed on the Templars. Bravely they fought and fell, but at last those who remained alive struggled through the opening and escaped to the army. Both the unsoldierly deed perpetrated, as also its speedy issue, greatly affected the standing of the Order. However, when the Moslem warriors rushed from the city's gates to charge the Christians, the remaining Templars pressed into the midst of the foe and fought savagely and untiringly until a complete victory was won. Ascalon capitulated immediately after the bloody battle, and Baldwin became master of the city in 1157 A.D. This city was held by the Christians until 1187, when the famous Kurd, Saladin, overwhelmed the crusaders. In 1270 the Sultan totally destroyed Ascalon, and filled its harbor with stones from its dismantled walls. Today broken pillars mark the location of what was a fortressed city. In the meantime the city of Tyre, the old opulent city of the Philistine or Phœnecian people, much referred to in the Hebrew Scriptures, had opened its ponderous gates to the Christian swordsmen. Battle followed battle throughout the reign of Jerusalem's king, while the two

Orders were constantly recruiting their war-wearing ranks by a stream of ambitious and sterling gentry from European countries. These few years, bloody though they were, summed up the hey-day of crusading success.

As it was wholly impossible to properly care for their ever-increasing landed estates in Europe, the liberal gifts of princely and baronial houses which counted it an honor in having sons as Knights in Palestine, Grand Commanderies, or rather Priories, were judicially instituted in various countries, constituting what was for centuries known as the Langues, that is, Languages of the Order of St. John. These were (1) Provence, (2) Auvergne, (3) France, (4) Italy, (5) Arragon, (6) England, (7) Germany. The Anglo-Bavarian language was afterwards substituted for that of England, and that of Castile added to the number. Priories in these countries were not instituted at the same time. A Priory, as the term implies, had *precedence,* was superior to any localized Commandery; in fact, it was an official union or correlation of provincial Commanderies.

Raymond du Puis died at the age of eighty years, 1160 A.D. The unexcelled historian of knighthood Orders, Major Porter, writes of this illustrious Master, "A true type of the soldier, the gentleman, and the Christian, he lived to see his every desire accomplished, and the Order in which all his ambition and all his hopes were centered take its place amidst the chivalry of Europe, upon the highest pinnacle reared by the hands of fame." Having overcome Palestine's Infidel rulers, had the Christian King sheathed his sword of conquest, as also the swords of the Knights, the rule of the Cross—the writer uses the term in its religio-military aspect—might have long continued in Palestine. But, alas! the lust for multiplied riches was the motive power, not, indeed, the mind and heart conversion of the Oriental tribes to the precepts and spirit of the cross-martyr, Jesus. Inveterate hatred of those men who respected and professed other teachings and religious leaders than those of the Latin Church bore its fateful fruit, death and destruction. The enlightened reader need not wonder at this, for few Christians in those times could read or write. Doubtless not one of a million ever so much as had in hands throughout life the Latin writings of the New Testament. Thus, then, it was these twain factors which spurred on the Christians to bloody encounters in distant realms of power. In 1162 the King of Jerusalem, stoutly backed by the valiant Orders of St. John and Templars, swept into the Caliph's sovereignty of Egypt to assist the Moslem in beating back the Turkomans who were devastating the country. Jerusalem's King was to receive a large annual tribute from the Caliph for his military aid. If the inconsistency of this enterprise was thought of, certainly the thought did not affect the king, or the Knights who assented to march with him. After one battle ensued, a peace was declared with the Turkoman leader. The youthful Kurdish prince, Saladin, who became afterward "the Napoleon of the East," was in this battle, and when peace was declared, he being enthused at beholding the conduct of the intrepid Knights, requested that he might receive the accolade. Saladin's request was granted, so we are told. This act, assuredly, was giving knighthood honor in an indifferent way. If it was the first o'erstepping of knighthood rule, manifestly enough, it was in no way the last. However, this sterling, intelligent Kurd prince was in every way, other than religion, worthy of such an honor.

Six years from this event, the King of Jerusalem proposed to the Grand Commander of St. John Knights that a real conquesting expedition into Egypt be made, although the Caliph "scrupulously observed" on his part the treaty and its tribute paying. The Grand Commander, d'Ascali, assented to the dishonorable undertaking, while, on the other hand, the Templars stoutly opposed it. The King's army was soon on the march, and in its first onset on a fortress it was victorious. Then with banners flying it swept toward Cairo, the principal city of Egypt. The Caliph was not idle in the meantime, but had despatched envoys to Noureddan the Turkoman leader to assist him against men who while they were great warriors did not hesitate, when mercenary motive prompted, to trample on a treaty. Noureddan required no second appeal sent him, so that he was soon swiftly speeding with a large army towards Cairo. When the Christian King discovered he ran the danger of being hemmed around he properly concluded to lift the siege and hurriedly return with his army to Jerusalem. It appears that the major membership of the Order of St. John felt that their Grand Master was wholly unworthy to retain his position in the Order's midst, hence he concluded to retire and return to Europe. Shortly afterward he was drowned in a shipwreck.

Later on by a few years, Saladin, who had become a worthy leader of the Turkoman army, burst suddenly from the south desert into Palestine, and in the quick onflow of eventuations a terrible conflict was waged on the shore of River Jordon. The two Orders were compelled to bear the brunt of the battle, and they were mercilessly cut to pieces. The Grand Master of St. John, an old tried crusader, although covered with wounds, swam his war-horse across the river, and escaped. The more unfortunate Grand Master of the Templars, after nobly beating down many a foeman, was captured. Doubtless he would have escaped had he not been unhorsed by the spearsmen of Saladin. It is recorded that in the furious moil of death-dealing blows there suddenly appeared a powerful Knight, astride of a milk-white horse, who seemed to fight with more than mortal strength. But he, too, fell, and the Turkoman warriors—horrible to relate!—drank of his blood, thinking that by so doing they would acquire his strength, and partake of his prowess and fighting worth.

With the coming of Saladin into war's arena the death-knell of Christian, rather, Latin, sovereignty in Palestine was sounded. As to whether the humiliating eventuality was a bane or a blessing, every enlightened mind must, perforce, tabulate its own verdict. In 1187 Saladin's army besieged the stronghold of Acre on the Palestine coast. Acre was the most opulent city of Palestine, and its fortifications were considered impregnable. The two Orders threw a very strong garrison of Knights into the city ere the Turkomans reached its walls. But all to no saving purpose were their herculean endeavours, their life-sacrificing night sorties. In one of these sorties they set on fire the Turkoman camp, and in the awful confusion which ensued, the Knights believed the hour of deliverance had come. But not so; Saladin appeared in person and rallied his myriad warriors to quick reprisals. What followed, the chronicler informs us,—"The Grandmaster of the Hospitallers repeatedly charged through the Saracen squadrons; but at length his horse received a wound which brought him down with his rider under him, and in a moment the venerable knight lay weltering in his blood, and hewn almost to pieces by the scimitars of the barbarians. The Hospitallers, when they saw him fall, formed a ring round his body; and it became the centre of a desperate conflict, in which many brave men of both armies fell."

The battle ended, however, without a decision of complete victory, as Acre still held against Saladin's entrance. He and his host retired from besiegement for the time being, and marched on the lake city of Tiberius. Here the King of Jerusalem with his brave Knights crossed swords with the determined Infidels. An awful conflict was waged, and its issue was a complete victory for Saladin. No less than thirty-thousand Christian warriors were slain, while the King of Jerusalem and the Grand Master of the Templars were made captives.

Now, indeed, the last days of the kingdom of Jerusalem were fast approaching. The Queen of Jerusalem desired to placate Saladin's wrath by the city's capitulation, but this proffer was peremptorily turned down. The Kurd prince demanded an unconditional surrender such as the crusade prince, Godfrey, had demanded of its Moslem Caliph. This the soldiery in the city stoutly refused, and besiegement was on. After fifteen days of besieging Saladin assented to the Queen's readiness to capitulate, and this was agreed to by the defending warriors. While, however, they expected merciless terms and treatment, Saladin as a conqueror surprised them. We are told, "The terms were at once honorable to the garrison, and indicative of a rare humanity in the conqueror. The city was left undespoiled, and the Christian nobles and soldiers were permitted to march out with their arms, and guaranteed a safe convoy to any town in which they might choose to seek refuge. As to the inhabitants, the native Greeks were allowed to remain unmolested; but such as were Latin by descent were required to pay a ransom, the men ten, the women five, and the children two crowns of gold, and to remove to some other place." Let the thoughtful reader balance in mind this Infidel prince's conduct when, some eighty years before, Jerusalem was torn from the Moslem Caliph, and within the sacred precincts of the Temple of Omar 10,000 citizens were mercilessly butchered. If human mercy to a fallen foe is a Christian virtue —and it is—then it must be confessed that this Kurd conqueror, this infidel Mohammedan, manifested more Christian virtue than did those who flauntingly professed to be soldiers of Christ. It indeed is the logic of history—however unpalatable the fact be—that those who profess the loudest are frequently those whose lives display the least of the spirit of their profession. It ever appears that the professional displayment is vised as the virtuous thing itself, while the genuine thing is indifferently ignored.

Saladin treated the Hospitallers in a kindly way. He gave ten of their number permission to tarry in the Hospital for a year, and thus care for the sick and wounded to their curing. Ere in person he entered the city, it is recorded that he "caused the bells of the Christian temples to be broken and melted down; and the Patriarchal Church, which had originally been a magnificent mosque, built by the Caliph Omar on the ruins of the famous Temple of Solomon, was carefully purified with rose water, and again dedicated to Infidel rites." Thus fell Jerusalem again into the possession of the Mohammedan warriors on October 2nd, 1187. Very properly has the historian queried, "Was it for this that Peter had, in the preceding century, thundered forth his denunciations against the Infidel, and aroused to a pitch of madness the enthusiasm of millions? Was it for this that Europe had poured forth her votaries, in countless hosts, to whiten the shores of Palestine with their bones?" No, it was not for this; but unholy ambition and greed bore such a harvesting.

CHAPTER VII

THE CRUSADE OF EUROPE'S KINGS, AND THE VICTORIOUS DELIVERANCE OF ACRE

> From shore to shore of either main
> The tent is pitched, the Crescent shines
> Along the Moslem's leaguering lines;
> And far and wide as eye can reach
> The turbaned cohorts throng the beach;
> And there the Arab camel kneels,
> And there his steed the Tartar wheels;
> The Turkoman has left his herd,
> The Sabre round his loins to gird.—BYRON

BOTH the princes and clergy of the Latin-churched kingdoms of Europe were distressed at the tidings that Jerusalem was again in complete control of the Infidel. But the Europeans, both at home and abroad, had justly none others than themselves to blame for the change of ownership. Had they been less covetous, more humanely disposed and considerate, and had, moreover, recognized the rights of those who in lineage, manners, religion, as also in language, differed from them, Jerusalem would have become a glorious Christian city, "whither the tribes go up," and in every way prosperous. As in a community when a man persists in outliving an over-bearing and hateful life, even to brutality, and is ever ready to rage upon those who choose to differ with his unmannerly conduct, such a fellow, sooner or later, must reap the just reward of his meanness; thus it is with a nation or an institution that chooses to play the role of an organized bully for the material riches which it purposes to secure.

> The mills of the gods grind slowly,
> Yet they grind exceeding small.

A new Crusade was voiced by kings and clerics alike, for we are told that Pope Urban III took the doleful news so keenly to heart that he died of grief. The Cardinals moaned out their woe in a very ostentatious manner, so much so that they voiced new vows as to pure living. As to this fact, an old time writer very aptly remarks that their vows "were like mariners' vows, they ended with the tempest." Men in those days were no more generously disposed to disgorge what they had grasped by hook or crook than the same class of men are today. History proves this as true. When many of the Latin citizens were expelled by Saladin from Jerusalem they found their way to Antioch which still was possessed by a European prince. They were denied the right of asylum by this autocrat, and, adding insult to injury, he robbed them of their personal possessions. However, this contemptible man speedily received his just deserts, for Saladin swept northward upon Antioch and wrung the rich city and Syria from his base clutch.

The good Archbishop of Tyre journeyed to Europe that he might, if possible, awaken the nations to action for the redemption of Jerusalem, but as a writer remarks, he found the "churchmen, one and all, far more ready to recommend the crusade to others, than to engage in it themselves." However, a conference of the princes was arranged, at which King Philip II of France, and Henry II of England, were present. Though these monarchs had no love for each other, yet they mutually decided to become allies in a crusade, in connection with the German Emperor, Frederick Barbarosa (the Red-haired), and the Austrian monarch.

Philip and Henry at once set about raising monies to properly equip large forces of warriors. Those of men, able-bodied, who chose to remain in their homes, were tithed one-tenth of their possessions. This subsidy was called "Saladin's Tithe." The King of Scotland paid Henry as a tithe five-thousand marks, no small sum in those days. The principal growlers against tithe payment, we are told, "were the religious communities" who had become rich by former crusaders' gifts in every country. Their insincere plea was that "princes ought to exact nothing from the clergy but continued prayers for the success of their arms." But such skim-milk disclaimers did not satisfy the monarchs, and they paid their apportionment, at least, it was taken from their holding. Henry died ere the armies were on their way, and sturdy Richard, his son, became King of England and Anjou. Richard, the Plantagenet, embarked from Dover in 1189 A.D. with 30,000 foot and 5,000 horse soldiery. King Philip had also recruited a large army. The elequent Archbishop of Tyre had traveled into Germany and Austria, and fired the Germans and Austrians with crusade enthusiasm. Powerful armies were soon on the march eastward, led by royal sovereigns. The Spanish monarchs required all their martial strength at home to guard against the Moslem Moors who were in possession of a large Spanish province. Still, the Queen of Arragon founded a beautiful monastery at Sienna and gave it to the Nun-Hospitallers who had lost their home in Jerusalem. In this they continued their virtuous labors.

The German Emperor, Frederick Barbarosa, while leading his army through Asia Minor, bathed in the Cydnus River, and the waters being cold by reason of the mountain snow, he took a sudden chill which speedily resulted in his death. This monarch was much beloved by his people, although he had stoutly quarreled with the Pope, yet he found that it was prudent, at least, politically, to conciliate the Pope. Ere he could be crowned by the Church, on his coronation day the Pope said to him, "You must prove yourself a faithful son of the Church by holding my stirrup while I mount." We are told that the Emperor reluctantly assented to the public humiliation. We read, "All was going smoothly; but the Emperor purposely mistook the stirrup. Then he growled out, 'I have yet to learn the business of a groom.'"

Richard of England was disappointed in getting away on ships with his army, and to add to his vexed spirit a fearful storm was experienced in voyaging. Two of his transports were grounded on the coast of Cyprus, a large island lying off the coast of Syria. This island is 150 miles in length, with an average breadth of 45 miles. The King of Cyprus, Isaac Comneni, cruelly treated the wrecked soldiery of Richard, and imprisoned them. When Richard reached Cyprus, hearing of Isaac's deed, as a lion he was enraged, and landing his men in the face of the Cyprian soldiery he fought this unprincipled enemy to a stand-still. Richard made a captive of Isaac, as also his daughter, and claimed Cyprus as his war-won possession. Isaac, it appears, much entreated Richard that he might not be disgraced by bonds of iron, hearing which Richard smiled and forthwith ordered chains of silver to be forged to bind the royal captive. As to this king, an Anglo-Norman monk penned, "He was the most wicked of men. He was said to be a friend of Saladin, and it was reported that they had drunk each other's blood, as a sign and testimony of mutual treaty." A word here as to this abominable custom of old. From history we glean that "a mode of allied friendship was for the two parties to open a vein and allow the blood to flow into the same bowl, mixing it thus together in token of union of lives. Sometimes wine was mixed with it and each drank the draught."

Prior to Richard's arrival in Palestine, the powerful fortress of Acre had been, time and again, stormed by the huge, though mixed army of crusaders. Yet no substantial results accrued to the besiegers, other than loss of men. There were intrepid Knights of both Orders, French, Flemish, Danish, Austrian, and German soldiery in the motley army, but this proved more a weakness than an advantage. In fact there had ensued jealousies, selfish wranglings, and harsh incriminations, among both princes and soldiers. What was needed was a bold, forceful uncompromising Napoleonic commander. Now King Richard of England and Anjou possessed these qualities, hence at his arrival matters quickly wore a more hopeful aspect. He was recognized as commander-in-chief.

In this connection it will be proper to call the reader's attention to the founding of the Order of Teutonic Knights. The German army had reached Acre in a woeful condition. It had fought its way through Asia Minor, not only against Turkomans, but with famine and pestilence. Upon its arrival a huge tent was erected, made up of ship sails, in which the wounded and diseased Germans were humanely cared for. In this army hospital was founded a knightly Order, exclusively Germanic. Pope Celestine III, in 1192 A.D. gave permission to found the Order according to the statutes of the Order of St. John, that is, both military and hospitallic. The Order of the Temple was but a religio-military order, it appears. The dress of the Teutonic Knights was a black dress, over which they wore a white cloak, with a black cross upon the left shoulder. We are told that "their clothes, armour, and the harness of their horses were all of the plainest description; all gold, jewels, and other costly ornaments being strictly forbidden. Arms of the best temper and horses of good breed were provided. When they marched to battle each knight had three or four horses, and an esquire carried his shield and lance."

When Richard landed at Acre he gave the keeping of the captive King of Cyprus to the St. John Knights. They possessed the fortified castle of Margat, not far distant. To the Knights of the Temple he sold the island of Cyprus for three hundred thousand livres. However, in after days the Templars returned it to Richard, as to them it proved more a bane than a blessing. If Richard returned to them their monies, or paid them a lesser price for it, to personal enrichment, no word is recorded.

At Richard's coming, all were heartened, although some princes were envious of him. How selfishly natural is this spirit! It is a weed in men's souls that remains vital throughout the centuries. It requires more than an assent to Church authority, or an adherence to and taste for high-class ceremonialism, to uproot it.

The English King set the pace to the goal of Acre's possession. What mattered it to this leonine warrior if Acre was stoutly manned with some of Saladin's choicest troops! This known fact was a spur to Richard's purpose. We are told that wherever a perilous service was to be performed, the war-cry of St. George for England resounded, and the crest (and, no doubt, the broom cockade) of the lion-hearted King constantly led the battle. The three military Orders were smitten with a noble envy of his valor, and rivaled each other in their exertions to be foremost in every assault. The Templars on one occasion lost their Grand-master; and of the Hospitallers, so many perished in their incessant conflicts with the enemy, that the Order would have been extinguished but for the crowds of young aspirants arriving from Europe, and who generally gave a preference to the banner of St. John. After terrible blood-shedding, on July 13, 1191, Acre was won over by the Christians. But, alas!

the great fortress was dearly purchased, for it was computed that more than one hundred thousand crusaders fell to rise no more. We may properly ask, was the cause worth such a human sacrifice? In a military aspect, of course, the test of strength between the East and the West was a blood-stirring drama to stage and enact; but, we may query, was such man-slaughtering of worth? True enough, the Latin Church was ready to exclaim, "It is the will of God!" But as Christians of today, after reading our Master's recorded words, can we soberly say such was the will of God?

The Knights of St. John moved their hospital from the castle of Margat to Acre where they took up abode after leaving Jerusalem. Richard marched to the deliverance of Cæsarea, Jaffa, and Ascalon. These cities were speedily repossessed and winter being at hand, that is, the rainy season, the soldiers became inactive. It appears that inaction did not produce good results, for certain leaders busied themselves in sowing dissatisfaction in the soldiers, and thousands marched to the sea-ports and embarked for Europe. As it was Richard's purpose to retake Jerusalem in the Spring, he seeing so many crusaders forsaking Palestine, exclaimed, "Those who are unwilling to rescue, are unworthy to view the sepulchre of Christ."

How keenly the lion-hearted King must have felt in beholding the troops thus turning their backs on captive Jerusalem! Every truly great man is sure to experience such unfraternal treatment. Aspersions are heaped upon him while living; and after he dies flowers will be placed on his grave.

After tarrying in Palestine some time after multitudes had sailed away, Richard, too, was impelled to hasten homeward, for report had reached him that prince John, his brother, was attempting to grasp his throne. Before leaving, however, he gave the island of Cyprus to Isaac's princess daughter as her marriage dowry, she, by Richard's planning, having married Jerusalem's professed king. It appears that Richard had a fondness for the princess and she for him. He gave to the Order of St. John his battle-won possessions in Palestine, thus making the Order a sovereign institution among the nations. The Order ever afterward was held as such.

Cœur de Lion—a name given Richard—entered into negotiations with Saladin, and a singular timed treaty of peace was agreed to, signatured by the two monarchs, and all the leading princes, both Christian and Infidel. The armistice was to continue for three years, three months, three weeks, and three days. These important matters being duly settled, Richard embarked and set sail for his home-land. It is recorded that as Richard stood on deck and watched the shore-line of Palestine receding, he impulsively outstretched his hands and exclaimed, "Holiest lands, I commend thee to God's keeping, and pray that he may grant me health to come and rescue thee from the infidel." But earnest-hearted Cœur de Lion never returned. A terrific storm wrecked the ship on the coast of Istria, and the monarch found himself in more danger on such land than he was on the raging waters. He knew the enmity of the Duke of Austria toward him, as also that of the German Emperor, Philip. However, he disguised himself, as best he could, and with his faithful page he started on his dangerous journey. When they reached Goritz, the king sent his page to the governor to secure a traveler's passport for "Hugh the Merchant." Richard gave a valued ring to the page to give to the greedy official. In doing this the king was indiscreet, and upon seeing the ring the Austrian was suspicious. The page hastened to the King and voiced his well-grounded fears, and they quickly moved forward. A Norman Knight was met with, who recognized Richard. He presented him with a horse, and the King took cheer. Alas, he was arrested and imprisoned. In a guarded castle he remained for months, until his place of confinement was discovered by a minstrel, a sincere friend of Richard, who had sought long to find him. By the castle's wall this man Blondel sang a stanza of a song he knew Richard loved. After singing it, he listened, and the King's voice was heard singing the following stanza.

> "Say what hast thou brought from the distant shore,
>   For thy wasted youth to pay?
> Hast thou treasure to win thee joys once more?
>   Hast thou vassals to smooth thy way?"
>
> "I have brought but the palm-branch in my hand,
>   Yet I call not my bright youth lost;
> I have won but high thought in the Holy Land,
>   Yet I count not too dear the cost."

The news of Richard's imprisonment traveled fast, and all Europe was stirred. The contemptible Duke now hurried his prisoner into Germany, and the German Emperor held him in duress, for months. In the meantime, the captive's Queen mother, Eleanor, urgently wrote letters to the Pope in behalf of her royal son, imploring him to command his just freedom. But the Pope in such a cause was dilatory. Queen Eleanor would not be balked in her righteous plea, and persisted in writing. It cannot but be interesting to the reader to peruse one of this mother's letters to the Pope, hence the author subjoins the following authentic epistle, "It is now the third time you have promised to send legates to procure the release of my son. If he were in property, we should see legates flying upon his first call, in hopes of being well rewarded by so generous a prince. Do you thus observe the promise you made us with the strongest protestations of friendship and affection? Do you thus deceive the simple, who put their trust in you? The most enormous crimes in the great and the powerful are connived at, and the rigour of the canons are only exerted against the poor. One tyrant keeps my son in captivity, while another invades and lays waste his dominions; the one holds, to use a vulgar expression, while the other flays. This the high pontiff sees, and yet keeps the sword of St. Peter in its sheath. Have we not too much reason to construe his silence into a tacit approbation and consent?" This letter is dated 1193 A.D. Such has too frequently been the dilatory method pursued by the Bishops of Rome throughout the centuries, especially in matters in and by which there may be a question whether benefits will accrue to them. This is the logic of history.

Return we now in our review to Palestine to scan briefly eventuations which in their passing compelled the European crusaders to bid farewell to the Holy Land. It transpired that the famous warrior, Saladin, outlived Richard but a few months. A slight wound he had received, gangrened, while he rested in Damascus, and thus his end came. An unbiased historian writes as to this princely Kurd, "A Kurd by nation, and habituated, from his infancy, to rely for advancement solely on his sword, he was singularly expert at all warlike exercises—a severe but generous commander, a just governor, and a humane man; qualities calculated to exalt him to a lofty station in a country where scarcely any virtue, save that of sheer valour in war, ever came to maturity . . . As he lived a hero, so, if his faith be not taken in judgment against him, did he die a righteous death. One of the last acts of his life was to order a considerable sum of money to be given to the poor of Damascus, without regard to creed; and, when he felt his end was approaching, an officer, in compliance with his orders, tore down his war pennon, and hung up his shroud in its stead, proclaiming to the populace as he did so, that in that melancholy garment they beheld all that the conqueror of the East could carry with him to the tomb."

Saladin never disregarded any treaty or mutual compact. This the Europeans had done more than once. Even King Richard's Truce, signed by crusade princes, was not allowed to terminate honorably, as to prescribed time, but was disregarded and o'erstepped. But, we may well ask, Of what availment? The answer is, only increased blood-shedding. It may have been that Saladin's sudden death was by the Christians considered proper reason to view the armistice as void, and as there ensued fratricidal warrings between his princely sons, after his passing, and, moreover, his cruel uncle, Saphadin, grasped sovereign prerogative, the newly arrived crusaders infringed on the Kurdish monarch's territory.

A writer has, in this connection, informed his readers that "the death of Saladin was hailed by the Latin Christians as a special interposition of Providence in their behalf." Alas, how senselessly prone are men to tabulate their own preferences and desires as bearing the sign-manual of the infinite God's approved will and decree! Can anything be more outrageously inconsistent and stupidly false? In this connection a brief statement as to the death of Richard will, doubtless, be of historic interest. Richard purchased his prison release and returned to England. His scheming brother, John, bent his knees before him and implored forgiveness. To the Queen mother Richard said, "I forgive him, and I hope I may forget the injury he has done me as easily as I know he will forget my pardon." It appears that a certain lordly vassal of Richard's, Vidomar Viscount of Limoges, France, found a treasure of ancient coins. Richard demanded this as his by royal right. The Viscount refused to assent to his monarch's demand, and Richard besieged the castle of Limoges. While Richard was riding beneath the castle's walls, a young man named Bertrand de Gourdon, a skilled archer, shot an arrow which fatally wounded the king in his shoulder. While Richard lay suffering, the castle was stormed and taken, and Bertrand was brought into the dying king's presence. Looking upon his enemy, the king said, "Knave, what have I done to thee that thou shouldest take my life?" The young man replied, "With thine own hands thou hast killed my father and my two brothers. Myself thou wouldst have hanged. Let me die now, by any torture thou wilt." Richard heard the condemning words, and said, "Youth, I forgive thee. Go unhurt!" Turning to his chief officer, the king said, "Take off his chains, give him a hundred shillings, and let him depart." Such were the last words of Richard Coeur de Lion, for after speaking he sank upon his couch and died. Alas! his generous command was not obeyed by his officer, for at his death Bertrand de Gourdon was flayed and brutally hanged. Alas for the crusaders! Their fortressed city of Jaffa was taken by assault, and no less than twenty thousand of their number were butchered.

The Hospital of St. John, throughout these years of battling and plundering, was located in Acre, and to show forth their sincere esteem for the Order, the populace changed the city's name to "St. John D'Acre." Ever afterward this famous city went by this name.

The professed King of Jerusalem and Cyprus, Amaury by name, found the citizens of Cyprus rebellious, he therefore, asked the Grand-Master of the Knight Hospitallers to send to Cyprus a company of Knights to quell the dissatisfied and quarrelsome natives, mostly Greek by lineage. This was done, and the Knights established themselves in Limisso, the chief city. Far better had it been if all the true and tried Knights in Acre had at this initial period located in Cyprus. However, if men of our day required an amazing surfeit of examples of past-time bravery, heroism, and self-sacrificing, then, indeed, such a surfeit was served up by those noble Knights. As they proved worthy of time-lasting renown, may we hope that their triumphant souls "go marching on." As there were established in European countries, as also in England and Scotland, Hospitals and Knight Priories of St. John, the Grandmaster at St. John D'Acre recruited his depleted company, prepared for continued warfare. At this epoch the Order was at its high-water mark of real estate possessions. It has been computed that at this time it claimed by right of indenture some 19,000 manors, while the Order of the Temple possessed some 9,000. These small landed estates were all gifts from the hands of admiring and heart interested friends. Doubtless it was true that this proof of preferential regard and esteem, as possessed at large, between the Order of St. John and the Templars, went far to cause envy and malice to enroot in unknightly hearts.

There is a point of history, little, if at all, touched upon by historical writers, which the intelligent and unbiased student should fix in mind relative to the Oriental armies which throughout those chivalric times warred incessantly against the inroads and onslaughts of the Crusade Europeans. It would be distinctly unjust and false to fact to foster the thought that all the various armies of the East were in spirit of one mischievous and desolating fabric. By no means were they so. The Moslem Arabians were a class of men by themselves; the Kurdish followers of Saladin were another; while, lastly, the deluging swarms of Korasmins, or Tartars, from the shores of the Caspian Sea, were distinctly another. These various peoples had little in common between them, although it is true that the far-flung teachings of the famous Arabian had more or less percolated into their minds, and controlled, in a way, their religious aspect of life. But, all in all, there was as great a distinction between them as today exists between the Irish and the English, or the New England Indian of 1620, and the Aztec of Mexico. These various Oriental warriors were not all savage and cruel in disposition, as biased Europeans adjudged them to be. In some important aspects they were the equals of the Christian warriors. In arts, sciences, and letters, they could, and in fact, did, teach the Europeans many things hitherto unknown to them. "Give the devil his due," is equitably proper in our judgment of men. There lies on the writer's desk, among other books, a volume of the writings of Persian poets. While these men lived and wrote five centuries earlier than Byron, Moore, and Burns, no modern poet has surpassed Firdausi, Sadi, Rumi, and Jami, although these literary adepts, even by name, are hardly known to westerners. It comes not amiss for the enlightened student to justly appraise this phase of historic knowledge. In much it ever has been men's willing ignorance of, and, moreover, readiness of mind to misjudge those who, from every view-point, are their equals, and, frequently, prove to be their superiors. Often is it the case that the howl of the wolf is camouflaged under the bleat of the sheep.

The Latin Church rulers were not content to have the monarchs of Europe become passive as to eastern conditions. So long as the crusade infection remained latent there was but little, if indeed any, self-sacrificing to be seen, hence to oppose this indifferent tendency another and still another crusade enthusiast arose and voiced the initial cry, *"Deus vult!"* Let it be noted, however, that the latter crusaders, led by their kings and princes, manifested a very loose disposition of mind and spirit as to who or what people they outpoured their militant vials upon. Thus it was that what is set down as the Fifth Crusade, began war operations to assist the Doge of Venice, Dandolo, to secure for himself the city of Zara on the Adriatic coast. Accomplishing with ease this unprincipled feat of arms, a youthful Greek Prince came into their midst and earnestly urged the crusading princes to set sail for Constantinople and pull from the throne his royal father's brother, who had villainously dethroned his parent, throwing him into a dark dungeon after tearing out his eyes. Of course, great riches were promised the Latins if they would assist to this righteous end! The crusaders readily assented to perform this work, and sailed for the city of Constantinople. While this was going on Palestine was bleeding from the merciless inroads of the Korasmins, a heathenish race of people. But it must be observed that all merciless villains were not housed or tented in the East. Well, the crusade army caused the base usurper of a brother's throne to row across the Bosphoros under cover of darkness and escape inflicted judgment. The eyeless Emperor was, together with his son, placed on his throne, while the imperial diadem was worn by the youth, as the father was a helpless invalid. Alas for peace and harmony! A vile monster, Mourzouffe by name, initiated a revolt in the imperial city, and soon had the youthful Emperor in a dungeon where the giant ruffian strangled him to death. Beyond the city walls the Europeans heard the murderous news, and a besiegement was on. For three months the army strove to hammer its way into the city of Constantine. Mourzouffe and his warriors held out against the besiegers. At last an escalade proved successful, and intense hand to hand fighting ensued. After a full day of conflict the ruffian leader fled, leaving behind his standard and heavy armor. The Latin princes chose one of themselves to be Emperor of the Greek dominions, and the Greek citizens had no voice in the choice, for in those times "might made right." The Latin soldiery in Constantinople committed every form of sacrilege, if the historian Gibbon has penned truly their conduct.*

All this amazing movement mightily pleased the Pope of the Latin Church, while, on the other hand, it was a deep humiliation to the Patriarch of the Greek Church. But all this action went not to the cause of Palestine's plight, not in the smallest degree. However, as we of today scan the raging doings of those blood-spilling times, we cannot but ejaculate: what mattered it whether the killings took place in St. John d'Acre or the City of Constantine? It ever has been that men of powerful placing who set about dealing out justice and executive judgment upon those whom they visé as their inferiors, while in some

* He writes, "the churches were profaned by the licentiousness and party zeal of the Latins. After stripping the gems and pearls, they converted the chalices into drinking cups; their tables, on which they gamed and feasted, were covered with the pictures of Christ and the saints. In the cathedral of St. Sophia, the ample veil of the sanctuary was torn asunder for the sake of the golden fringe; and the altar, a monument of art and riches, was broken in pieces and shared among the captors. A prostitute was seated on the throne of the patriarch; and that daughter of Belial, as she is styled, sung and danced in the church, to ridicule the hymns and processions of the Orientals."

enactments they may be just, too frequently prove themselves to be despotic, sordidly unjust, and, in fact, enemies of impartial and ennobling justice.

The state of conditions in Palestine remained the same, if not growing more and more dangerous and theatening. Deep distrust, in truth, fateful enmity was shown by both St. John and Templar Knights toward and for each other. Not even the Pope was able to eradicate this virulent spirit from the Orders, although official effort was put forth. To mention this historic fact is the duty of the writer, however much he deplores the fact. The Fifth Crusade ended with its purpose unachieved; a sixth militant uprising under the command of John de Brienne, a real knightly warrior, was forthwith launched. To place him in full prominence he was married to the so-called Queen of Jerusalem. Noting the helplessness and pressing danger of the Christians who tarried in the few fortressed cities of Palestine, Brienne implored Pope Innocent III to bestir the European monarchs to engage in another crusade. The Pope was quite willing to do so, hence a general council was held in Rome. Innocent emulated the example of his predecessor, Urban II, and eloquently voiced the need of Palestine and the Holy City. The old cry, *"Deus Vult!"* again resounded. It appears that the Pope was afraid of the territorial power of the German Emperor, Frederic, for he considered that the Emperor encroached on his Italian states. To Innocent's mind Frederic was dilatory as to embarking with his army and knights, although he had vowed to engage in the movement. The Pope attempted to hurry away the royal German, but he stoutly refused to be dictated to by the Pope. We pause to query: where is he who possesses warm red blood coursing in his veins, and who prizes the consciousness that he is a free man, who will condemn Frederic for his refusal to up and away at the behest of a fellow mortal? However, we are told that "priestly craft achieved what reproaches could not compass. It was proposed that, being a widower, he should marry Violante, only daughter and heiress of the King of Jerusalem." Thus it was that the magnetic pull of a woman to marital bonds, was more powerful than the Pope's commanding utterances. The Emperor agreed to embark in two years, as he required such time to rightly prepare, as also settle sovereign affairs in Europe. When the years passed, he wrote the Pope his need of some time extension. Such was agreed to, seeing he had married Violante. At last he embarked, which much pleased the troubled Pope. But, alas! when not far on the sea, Frederic became quite ill,—a *mal-de-mer*, perhaps,—and he returned to the port of Tarento. The up-shot was, the Emperor was excommunicated from the Church as an unholy reprobate. This was a serious blow to Frederic, and regaining normal health, he again embarked as a crusader, with forty thousand men, but the Pope was determined to subdue or crush him. An envoy was speeded away to St. John d'Acre to inform the Knights, as also people, that he was outside the Christian Church. The Emperor arrived in Palestine before the envoy, and the Christians rejoiced in his powerful presence; but when the envoy appeared, and the excommunication was known all the Knights but the Teutonic stood aloof from him. But the sturdy Frederic moved forward, bent on Jerusalem's liberation, and though the two Orders felt subject to the Pope's decree, they could not see the Emperor's army moving without mounting their horses and following in the rear. It was well they did, for they found much to do in beating off the harassing enemy. Frederic in magnificent assault snatched the Holy City from the Turkoman force within, as also other fortresses yielded to his power.* But while Frederic was striking the foe in Palestine, the Pope in Europe was bringing troops into his dominions to tear to pieces his imperial sovereignty. The reader can judge who of the two sovereigns was the sincerest crusader. By previous agreement, Jerusalem's crown was to be worn by Frederic, and

* The Emperor entered Jerusalem March 17, 1229. He signed a treaty of peace with the Sultan for ten years from the date of entrance. This treaty, like Richard's, was broken by the Europeans, to their own utter undoing and banishment.

he had won it. However, the Church Patriarch refused to coronate him, so he himself took the emblem in hand, and, handing it to the Grandmaster of the Teutonic Knights, the latter placed it on his head as lawful King of Jerusalem. After some time, Frederic embarked for Europe, and upon his arrival, the Pope hurled a bull against him, declaring therein that in the name of God all his subjects were freed from his authority. This was too much for the persecuted Emperor to endure, so he had no other alternative than to throw himself on the mercy of his powerful enemy. A huge payment of monies was levied to his account, viz., 100,000 ounces of gold. This he paid in full, and the Church's curse was declared null and void. It will be proper, in connection with this brief historic survey, to query: who of these two men hindered the emancipation of Palestine? Had the two stalwart Orders felt free to throw their full fighting strength into the balance with Frederic, as they had some years before with Richard, of a certainty much more effective results would have been accomplished. Granted that the Emperor was headstrong, was there not another than he, who, if history be authentic, possessed a full measure of this ingredient? All in all, if any living man inherits sovereign prerogative, it roots in an impartial and untainted man-to-man equity and unselfishly balanced justice. The autocrat—whether political or religious—is in make-up a bi-product from selfish ingredient. Jesus the Nazarene was in no way or measure a quarreler with the kings of earth, nor did he delegate his disciples to do so. Surely it is of moment to take note of this fact.

At this epoch the Order of St. John was throughout Europe at the high-water mark of wealth in landed estates, as also in man power. Its numerous hospitals, constituting priories, were depots from whence the parent Priory in Palestine drew recruits for constant warfare.

The Seventh Crusade succeeded the conquests and adventures of Frederic, and we are credibly informed that "among others, there went from the house of the Order in Clerkenwell, London, three-hundred knights, preceded by Theoderic their prior, at the head of a considerable body of armed stipendaries. They marched with the banner of St. John unfurled before them; and as they passed over London Bridge, saluted, with hood in hand, the crowds who congregated to see them depart... As to the Chapel or House of Clerkenwell, London, it was founded in the twelfth century, and dedicated by Heraclius, Patriarch of Jerusalem, when he visited England as ambassador in 1115. It was the principal house of the Order in England." Alas! few, if any, of the Anglo-Saxon Knights returned to their home-land.

Some fifteen years passed by from the day that Frederick had entered Jerusalem, and in their passing the treaty of peace had been disregarded by the Christians. This fact stirred the Sultan to secretly invite the Korasmin leader to sweep down upon Jerusalem and destroy the Latins. The Christian Orders, by some means, found out the secret pact, and enjoined the citizens to flee to Jaffa on the near coast. But many of the people imposed faith in the battling strength of the brave knights of the Cross, and ignored the warning word. Alas! such citizens as remained— and they were many—were shortly hacked to pieces by the merciless enemy. Jerusalem was stormed, entered, and utterly despoiled. The Orders quickly recruited their shattered ranks, and shortly after faced the cruel foe near the city of Gaza. Though their valor was glorious, and their blows death-dealing, they were outnumbered twenty to one, their brutal adversaries laughed at death, and pressed them to defeat. We are told that "the Grandmasters of the Hospital and Temple, and the Commander of the Teutonic Order, were all slain, and there escaped from the sword of captivity only thirty-three Templars, sixteen Hospitallers, and three Teutonic knights." Thus fell Jerusalem, after streams of European blood crimsoned the soil of Palestine.

As if Providence interposed to save the remnant of Christians who remained in St. John d'Acre, a fierce fratricidal feud suddenly ensued in the army of the Korasmins, and, like destructive locusts, they swept away.

After these tragic events, another crusade to slay the Infidel was initiated by King Louis IX of France. His consort being seriously ill, he vowed if she recovered he in person would lead an army against the Infidel. As she regained her health, Louis began to prepare to make good his vow by recruiting sixty thousand fighting men. When all was orderly arranged, the King embarked his army on 180 vessels and pointed his course for Cyprus. Though Henry III of England agreed to head an army together with Louis, he failed to go in person, but a valiant warrior, William Longsword, embarked with a strong company of knights in his stead. This company joined arms with the French at Cyprus, and also the two Orders of brave knights were quick to join the new adventure. After some time spent on the island, the army embarked for Egypt, determined to strike the Sultan lion—or, dragon,—in his very den. The city of Damietta was easily stormed, and dropped like a ripened apple into hand. The Europeans moved onward, finding the rich country depopulated, and, strangely enough, not a Moslem warrior in sight. Veteran knights were suspicious as to what this void did portend, but galloped onward in the van. The upshot was, the astute leader of the Moslem forces was weaving a web in which to entrap the proud Louis and his army. In this he succeeded to the utter defeat and blasting of the western leader's ambition and purpose. The food rations of the army failed, and in the many sluggish water-ways the soldiers caught thousands of eels and converted them into food. Alas, they but poisoned their blood, for these eels had been fattening on the putrid corpses of men who had been slain by the crusaders' swords in and around Damietta. Such poisonous food produced a plague which depleted their ranks by thousands, and when they came face to face with the Moslem soldiery, their defeat was inevitable. It appears that the heady Count of Artois disapproved of the plan of action voiced by William Longsword, the English knight, and exclaimed sneeringly, "Behold the cowardice of these longtails!" To this Longsword replied, "I will go so far into danger, that you will not even dare to touch my horse's tail." And, indeed, this brave English knight did this, and died with his face to the foe, and his blood-dripping sword in hand, while this conceited Count was taken a captive, together with King Louis and his gentry. Almost every St. John knight, as also those of the Temple, fell in death, preferring death to humiliating imprisonment. The Sultan levied a ransom of 800,000 besants (£16,000) on Louis and his men, which great liberating sum the King borrowed from the two Orders. A treaty of peace was duly signed, and Louis set sail for St. John d'Acre. He remained in Palestine some time, then re-embarked for Europe.

Still another crusade was launched by the English and the French in 1270. The French King planned to strike the Moslems on the African coast at Tunis and Carthage. The plan was suicidal to Louis and many of his men, for a pestilence swept upon them, and the ambitious King became one of its first victims. This French monarch was canonized into a Saint by Pope Boniface VIII, and today one of America's great cities bears his name, "St. Louis." Prince Edward of England sailed for Palestine with seven thousand men. The Orders of Knights joined with him, and some minor successes followed. At Jaffa the Prince was taken sick, and while lying on his couch, a Moslem came desiring an interview with him, saying he had very important news to communicate. The interview was granted, and in conversation with Edward, the base assassin suddenly drew his dagger and stabbed the prince, yet not fatally. The prince sprang up, and floored the assassin, and forcing the weapon out of his grasp, plunged it into his enemy's heart. The story went that Queen Eleanor sucked the poison from the wound. As to this, a quaint English writer remarks, "It is showed how Eleanor, his wife, sucked all the poison out of the king's wound without doing any harm to herself: so sovereign a remedy is a woman's tongue, anointed with the virtue of loving affection." Edward recovered from both wound and illness, and returned to England. The King, his father, having died while he was sailing homeward, upon his arrival he was crowned King.

The last crusade host had gone to Palestine, although, as usual, the reigning Pope put forth an effort to interest anew the monarchs. The effort was futile, as, indeed, any continued effort was senselessly inconsistent. The Europeans who remained in Palestine resorted to the double-walled city of St. John d'Acre for safety. But the Egyptian Sultan determined upon utterly outrooting the Europeans from Syria, and Palestine. He was well assured that so long as they were subject to the Latin Church's Bishop there could ensue no peace. As to this, he judged rightly. Antioch was first enveloped by a mighty army of Mamalukes, and speedily fell to the Sultan. In its taking, seventeen thousand citizens were slaughtered, and one hundred thousand taken captive, to become slaves. After Antioch's overthrow, a mighty army of sixty thousand horsemen, and one hundred and forty thousand infantry, pressed forward to the walls of Acre. Sadly true it was that this fortressed city was rife with every unspeakable immorality. Licentious debauches, it appears, had taken up residence in the fated city, as if it was Heaven's will to use the enemy to rid the earth of such human vermin. The Knights of the three Orders strove to stay the unholy proceedings, but to little avail. Within the fortress there were twelve thousand knights, and they determined to repel the mighty enemy or die in the city's defence. No mortal pen can set forth the horrors of the drawn-out deathly struggle. The hot air became tainted with the odor from putrifying bodies, both without and within the walls. At last the Sultan's miners burrowed beneath the mighty stone towers, and one after the other fell, burying deeply hundreds of valiant knights who had manned them. As to the tragic ending of the Latin power in Palestine in the fall of St. John d'Acre, the words of a crusade historian will be submitted as a proper ending of this dramatic chapter. "Sixty thousand persons perished within the walls, or were carried into slavery; and the Sultan, to annihilate forever the hopes of the Christians of effecting a new settlement on the Syrian shore, razed the fortifications of every city on the coast. Thus terminated, in blood and desolation, a war, which had lasted, with little interruption, for one hundred and ninety-four years, and which retains the appelation of 'Holy' to this day;—a war," says the chronicler, "for continuance the longest, for money spent the costliest, for bloodshed the cruelest, for pretences the most pious, for the true intent the most politic, the world ever saw."

After Acre's fall, those few knights who survived embarked for Cyprus. In our survey we will, in the ensuing chapter, follow the battle-scarred heroes.

CHAPTER VIII

THE KNIGHTS OF ST. JOHN AT CYPRUS AND RHODES

> "And on his breast a bloodie crosse he bore,
> The deare remembrance of his dying Lord,
> For whose sweete sake that glorious badge he wore,
> And dead, as living, ever Him adored.
> Upon his shield the like was also scored,
> For sovereign hope which in his help he had;
> Right faithful true he was in deed and word."

BEFORE the reader's attention be called to consider the stirring movements of the Knights Hospitallers apart and away from Palestine, the writer deems it of interest to the reader to state briefly that in very little were the Latins of Europe benefited by years of contact with Eastern peoples. Not because they might not have been, but rather because they chose to remain ignorant of much in which the Orientals were far in advance of them. In much they were stupidly purblinded by their servile devotion to their religious lords. Thus it ever was and is that

> He who's convinced against his will,
> Is of the same opinion still.

A profound scholar in writing as to the mental status of the Latins, Greeks, and Arabians, remarks, "If we compare, at the era of the crusades, the Latins of Europe with the Greeks and Arabians, their respective degrees of knowledge, industry, and art, our rude ancestors must be content with the third rank in the scale of nations." We ask: is it justice to Christianity to declare that mental virility and breadth, together with that which means refinement, must be the fruit of other teaching than that of the school of Jesus the divine Master? Clearly, to the writer of this treatise, such tones not of justice or properly imposed merit. If indeed the precious diamond be buried from men's admiring vision, and in its place a paste bauble be held up to sight, if then the pretentious baked thing be proved to be inferior in prismatic radiation to others, it would but dishonor the buried diamond to hold that the counterfeit stone, however resplendent its setting, must be recognized as the true original. We are further told that "in a reign of sixty years, the Latins of Constantinople disdained the speech and learning of their subjects; and the manuscripts were the only treasures which the natives might enjoy without rapine or envy." Need it be remarked that the greatest bane of mankind, in every land, is mental enslavement to the teachings of weedy superstitions? However, it is a cheering fact that there inheres in the souls of men a diviner light and principle, which, in a measurable degree, o'erbounds all benighting thoughts, and makes to heroism, to nobility of conduct, in truth, makes the gentleman. So have we found of the past; so it is of to-day.

When St. John d'Acre fell into the Sultan's grasp, the remnant of valiant knights, as has already been stated, sailed for Cyprus taking with them all the archives of the Order. The King of Cyprus had been in St. John d'Acre, he and his soldiers, assisting in the deathly struggle, but to his discredit, under cover of dark night he had deserted the defenders and sailed homeward. Upon the arrival of the few war-wounded veteran knights of the two Orders, he was graciously kind and obliging, and in generous behaviour gave to them the city of Limmisa as a dwelling place. The few Teutonic knights who escaped from Mamaluke butchery embarked for Germany where they found true friendship and good cheer. The Hospitaller Commander, brave John d'Villiers, despatched letters to all the Priories of Europe to send at once recruits to Cyprus. His orders were promptly acceded to, and soon he had all the knights he required for future movement and using. This fact, it appears, was noted by the King of Cyprus, and his greedy disposition, in union with suspicious fears, led him to deny the Grand-Master the privilege of purchasing any Cyprus real estate. Not only so, but he had the audacity to levy a poll-tax on the Order's members. The fruit of all such tyranny ripened speedily. His Cyprian citizens initiated a revolt, and the King was made a prisoner. To rid the island of him, they deported him to Cilicia in Asia

THE ISLAND OF CYPRUS

Minor. The exiled monarch's brother was enthroned in his seat, yet he had no more than taken authority when he was stabbed through the heart by a political friend of the deposed exile. Truly did the pen of Shakespeare write:—

> Princes have but their titles for their glories,
> And outward honor for and inward toil.

Strange and inconsistent as it may appear to the reader, it is nevertheless historic fact that the man who was Pope at this time, Boniface VIII, received an envoy from the Mogul Prince, a Tartar chieftain, who was an enemy of the Sultan, asking the Pope to raise an army as an ally of his own, and thus together crush the Sultan's power. The Tartar Prince agreed to give the Pope full possession of Palestine and Syria. The Pope coveted this enriching prize, hence, being an autocratic man in temperament, he sent King Philip of France a command to recruit at once a large army for crusade enterprise. Philip sourly dissented, and dismissed the Pope's nuncio from his presence. This, of course, could not be countenanced by Peter's professed successor, hence a quarrel was on. As the Order of the Templars was more powerful in France than elsewhere in Europe, and, moreover, as both knighthood Orders were subject to the Pope, Philip surmised that the Templars were hand-in-glove with Boniface in his autocratic demand, hence hate took deep root in his heart toward the enriched Order.. This Pope died shortly after this rupture, and Philip played Church politics by having a leading cleric secretly agree to his purpose and plan, if the influence of the King would place him in Peter's seat. This cleric won out, and he took the name of Clement the Fifth.* Becoming Pope, he despatched letters to the Grand-masters of both Orders to appear speedily in their persons before him for an interview of importance, viz., the coalescing of the Orders into one, as also a possible movement against the Infidel. It appears that the Grand-master of the Hospitallers had misgivings that all was not revealed or set forth, for with other words the Pope wrote, "come speedily, with as much secrecy as possible, and with a small retinue." Grand-master Villiers was aboard his galley when the Pope's envoy reached him, and having in mind great plans for his Order's future, he felt no desire to set sail for Europe, hence he wrote the Pope to excuse him for the time from breaking away from urgent duties which demanded his time and mind. At the same time he addressed a fraternal

* In corroboration of what the author has stated, he submits the like statement from the learned author of the book, "The Knights Templars," Sir C. G. Addison. He writes, "he (Philip) succeeded, through the intrigues of the French Cardinal Dupré, in raising the Archbishop of Bordeaux, a creature of his own, to the pontifical chair. The new Pope removed the Holy See from Rome to France. Of the ten new Cardinals created, nine were Frenchmen, and in all his acts the new Pope manifested himself the obedient slave of the French monarch."

letter to the Grand-master of the Templars, Jacques de Molai, urging him to remain and join arms with him in capturing the beautiful island of Rhodes, as this, of all things, appeared to him to be the important conquest to achieve. Molai by letter thanked Villiers, and concluding his reply wrote, "We have both our duties, and you must cleave to your knights, and I to mine. Yet all you say affects me. No doubt of wealth and honor; but what are they to produce? Farewell."

This was a fateful choosing on the part of the Templar Grand-master, not only for himself, but for his valorous Order. He forthwith sailed from Cyprus with his knights, carrying with him 150,000 florins of gold, together with a vast amount of silver money, the whole requiring twelve horses to carry. Very unwisely did the Grand-master deposit this metallic wealth in the Temple in Paris. Little did Molai dream of the atrocious and deadly plot which the impious King, seconded by his heartless minions, was secretly hatching to the Order's destruction, as also the terrible deaths of himself and his brave companions in arms. But so it was. The writer will not dwell in any full way upon the voracious cupidity, infamous craft, and merciless enactments of the French king and his basely unholy minions, both of Church and State. Suffice it to say that on October 13, 1307, all Knights of the Temple in France were arrested, and 900 were immured in prisons. No less than 140 knights were put to the torture in Paris, and thirty-six of the sufferers died. After spending five years in a dungeon, Jacques de Molai, the noble Grand-master of an illustrious Order, together with a company of his eminent Companions, suffered death by fire at the will of their traducers. When chained to the stake of burning, the Grand-master exclaimed, "The decree which condemns us is an unjust decree, but in heaven there is an august tribunal to which the weak never appeal in vain. To that tribunal within forty days I summon the Roman Pontiff." A violent shudder ran through the crowd, but the Grand-master continued, "O Philip, my master, my King! I pardon thee in vain, for thy life is condemned. At the tribunal of God, within a year, I await thee." Startling the historic fact that both Pope and King died shortly after this appalling tragedy!

Return we now to our study of the Knights Hospitallers in Cyprus. Such an Order of intrepid men could not endure to remain in inaction, content to hold and luxuriate on the vast properties possessed in Europe. If the knights had concluded to do this, putrifaction would have speedily ensued, for nothing is more potent for baleful effects than human indolency. The knowledge as to the Christian kingdom of Jerusalem having passed away did not deter Europeans from persisting in pilgrimaging. It was to many, doubtless, a good way to declare life riddance of home unpleasantnesses, and, it may be, legitimate debts contracted. To thus become "a pilgrim" wiped the slate clean. Though the dangers of such journeying had not lessened by the over-land route, the Grand-Master of the Hospitallers had in the meantime fitted up the Order's galleys as transports and engaged them in carrying pilgrims between Italian ports and the Syrian shores. While thus engaged, the Knights learned that a vicious swarm of corsair galleys were ploughing the sea, intent on robbery and murder. The Grand-Master's own galley had been considered a prize worth taking, but in the naval encounter the knights had bested the pirate enemy. Here, then, was stirring enterprise for the Order, hence wholeheartedly the brave knights sprang to their work on the seas. The Order could not with satisfactory ease of mind remain long on the island of Cyprus. As men whose spirits disdained meannesses of over-bearing conduct they, as a sovereign Order by legal right, felt the need of a territorial home, freed from sordid interferers. Thus it was that in the Grand-Master's sailings, to and fro, he had often gazed with delight upon the charming island of Rhodes. He had informed himself as to its history. Not only so, but as a writer has penned, "Rhodes, from its proximity to Palestine, and the excellence of its port, was the point to which their views were ultimately directed. That island was, at that time, inhabited partly by Greeks, and partly by Turks and Saracens, whose corsairs the native princes openly sheltered from the pursuit of the Christian galleys." Grand-Master Villiers having died, William de Villaret was chosen to fill the very responsible office. He heartily entered into the well-planned enterprise which his wise predecessor had conceived. Letters were sent to the various Priories of Europe as to a very important undertaking about to be launched, hence those of brawn and nerve who were willing to serve the Order, in life or death, were called upon to report in person at the Italian port of Brundusium. A few princes, as also the Pope, was made knowing as to the purpose in mind, and hearty acquiescence prevailed. As a prophecy of success the Grand-Master pleasingly found when his transports sailed into Brundusium that there were awaiting his arrival a two-thirds over-plus of fighting men. Taking, however, as many as space and wisdom warranted, the fleet sailed out of port early in the spring of the year 1308. As far as the soldiery aboard, both knights and military citizens, were concerned, the fleet was sailing under sealed orders, although all had in mind the storming of some eastern port as a new crusade movement. When the real purpose of the expedition was voiced to them, there ensued no whisper of dissatisfaction: all alike were pleased.

In this connection a brief description of Rhodes will be enlightening. "It is about one hundred and twenty miles in circumference, and divided from the continent of Asia Minor by a channel twenty miles broad. The climate is delicious:— the summer being free from intense heat, and the winter mild and humid. The soil is singularly fertile, and produces fruits in abundance. Wild roses hang around the base of the rocks; beds of flowering myrrh perfume the air; and tufts of laurel-roses adorn the banks of the rivulets with their gaudy flowers." Sailing to Cyprus, the fleet took on board all the knights stationed there, together with the property and archives of the Order. Thus it was a glad farewell to Cyprus forever, and its sordid king. From Cyprus the fleet sailed to the coast of Lycia and anchored, to await the arrival of certain spies whom the Grand-Master had prudently sent to Rhodes to secure information as to the most vulnerable vantage point to land his forces, as also to discover the possible strength of opposition which would have to be overcome. When the spies arrived, the fleet sailed out to sea and trimmed its sails towards Rhodes. Greatly were the natives of the fair island surprised at the great fleet's sudden appearance, and the quick disembarkment that followed. However, surprise soon gave place to wrath, and the struggle for mastery was on. The Greek Emperor at Constantinople soon heard of this bold and as he considered it, piratical, landing upon his territorial claim, hence he despatched a powerful body of troops to co-operate with the Rhodians to beat back to sea the Latin intruders. Now the aggressors had their warring mettle put to the test, for skirmish followed skirmish, while days of struggle lengthened into two full years, in the passing of which hundreds of both contending soldiery were slain, as also other hundreds of the Latins deserted—not, indeed, the Hospitaller knights—and surreptitiously sailed homeward. Grand-master Villaret, however was determined to have and to hold the Island of Rhodes or leave his corpse—like others of his death-struck companions—upon its soil. At last he chose to strike at the city of Rhodes, a city of old historic wealth and renown. But the possession of the city was no easy task to accomplish, for a desperate conflict soon ensued which, for a long time, continued. As to this conflict we are told by the historian that "the Grand-master beheld the bravest of his knights hewn down before his eyes; but victory ultimately declared for his banner; and the Saracens, totally routed, threw themselves into their galleys, and carried to the Lycian shore, and the islands of the Archipelago, the first news of their defeat. Availing himself of the panic this event occasioned among the troops that garrisoned the city, the Grand-master stormed the outworks. Amid a shower of arrows and other destructive missiles, his knights gained the breach, and on the 15th of August, 1310, planted the standard of the Order permanently on its walls."

After the taking of the city of Rhodes, and the subjugation of the island's citizen population, the Grand-master manned his galleys and sailed to achieve conquests in other places. In this expedition he brought under the Order's power the small islands of Nisara, Lero, Calamo, Episcopia, Chalce, Simia, Tilo, and Cos. The last mentioned was the greatest value of the number, and to the Order was an important possession. It has been a matter of surprise to the author of this treatise to discover in his extensive researches that the monumental history of Edward Gibbon sets forth but an exceedingly brief allusion to the Knights of St. John, known as the Knights of Rhodes, after the Order fixed its chief residence on the beautiful island. But that which this great writer has penned regarding its long continued residence tones not disparagingly. Writing as to the subjugation of various countries to the enslaving power of the Ottoman Turks, Gibbon declares, "The servitude of Rhodes was delayed two centuries by the establishment of the Knights of St. John of Jerusalem; under the discipline of the Order, that island emerged into fame and opulence; the noble and warlike monks were renowned by land and sea, and the bulwarks of

Christendom provoked, and repelled, the arms of the Turks and Saracens." True and laudatory though the words of the great historian ring, every student of history has learned that it is not a strong qualification of human nature to retain consistent poise when a whole park of praises is shot at him or them. Man glorification, as a general thing, is more effective in deteriorating than in enhancing the worthiness of him or them who receive the glory. Many a man has been irreparably side-tracked into the pestilent bog of vain conceit by seductive flattery. All Europe rang with loud acclaim of glory and praise to the Knights of St. John for their illustrious achievement; and, moreover, on the other hand, the sterling, chivalric, and fighting deeds of the Knights of the Temple were ignored, and their Order defamed, despoiled, and destroyed. At a council of Pope and bishops in 1311, the disposition of the Templars' property was that "the confiscated property should be consecrated to the defence of the holy places (a very elastic and indefinite phrase), and that the Knights of Rhodes should have the unrestrained administration of it." Now from the mental viewpoint of the writer of this historic sketch, it would have been eminently consistent had the Grand-master of the Order of St. John peremptorily refused to enact any part in the property using or holding. As the entire tragedy from its hate-hatched inception reeked with wickedness, this vote as to "unrestrained administration" deserved absolute rejection, as also denouncement as an insult to the Order of St. John. But such was not done, for the reason, perhaps, that the Christian conscience was much smudged and atrophied in those property-stealing times, times when professed Christians were notorious despoilers of the rights of their fellow-men.

This enclothement with increased properties, in a double measure, could not do else than work detrimentally to the morally wholesome code and meritorious discipline of the Order. History clearly avers that such a deterioration ensued shortly following what has been narrated. We read, "The vast accession of wealth, conjoined with the conquest of Rhodes, raised the Order of St. John to a degree of splendor and renown which no military fraternity had ever before attained. But increase of revenue, and of popular acclaim, had a blighting influence on those very virtues which had led to this pre-eminence. Europe poured the younger sons of its aristocracy into the White Cross ranks; and with these high-born aspirants for knightly honours, came pride and luxury, and arrogance and disunion—the very sins that had prostrated the Templars in the dust. The statute enforcing community of property was permitted to become obsolete—while the younger knights, regarding valiant deeds on the deck of their war-galleys as the only duties imperatively required of them, squandered, in gaming and debauchery the spoil which they tore from the Infidels on the waves."

By painstaking research the student who scans the degenerate times of European history, especially of the Order of St. John, cannot do else than place the blame for laxity of morals and disrespect for the Order's statutes upon the Grandmaster, Villaret. Hardly would it have been possible for a Mogul chieftain or a Moslem Sultan to outvie him in luxurious living. Nothing of the mind and spirit which actuated and controlled the Order's earlier Masters was shown by him. His example was in every way injurious to the youthful knights, and the older veterans who openly protested against violating conditions were accounted testy babblers. Such a lawless spirit brought its own revolting reward. The loose living of the Knights of Rhodes—the name which the Pope now gave them—began to be much talked about in Europe, and, knowing this, the knights who loved the Order and valued its illustrious reputation rebelled against Villaret, and he slipped away out of the city to a fortress castle some leagues distant, and there surrounded by knights of like desires, bade defiance to all others. As such a state of affairs was suicidal to the Order, the Pope was appealed to as a last resort, and he with politic alacrity took the matter in hand.

He sent a message to Villaret to come to him and make known to him his side of the serious dissension and revolt. Villaret obeyed the Pope's summons, and a council was held. The result was that in name Villaret to his life's close should retain the title, Grand-master, yet a competent knight should at Rhodes fill the office, yet in no way subject to Villaret's prerogative or interference. Moreover, Villaret should not tarry at Rhodes, but reside in a priory in Europe, with all the comforts of life. Thus the reader can see how this man filled the position of a modern *pastor-emeritus*, as duly recognized in some church bodies. Now the astute Pope did not conclude his arranging and rectifying with the placing of Villaret where his influence was null, but he set forth that at Villaret's death the Pope should choose his successor to the office of Grand-master. This was a papal encroachment upon the Order's original statute. If assented to it would make the famous Order a mere puppet of the Pope's rule and possession. Prudent knights opposed this scheme of action on the clear ground that the statutes of the Order forbade it, and, besides, the sovereignty of the Order disallowed outside jurisdiction and authority. The Pope knew all this, yet he did not hesitate to nullify statutes if in doing so he could increase his own power over institutions, however foundationed they were. Though he did not press the matter to official demand, he astutely stated his preference of a knight to fill the position in Rhodes in the life-time of Villaret. The knights in conclave assented to the Pope's choice, Helion de Villeneuve. This man was, of course, extremely pleased with the Pope's spoken regard toward him, and about the first official act he performed was to present the Pope a landed possession near Cahors which, it appears, was much desired by the Holy Father of Christendom. Villeneuve, however, creditably set about rectifying flagrant abuses in the Order, as the records attest. We are told that "it was ultimately decreed that a certain term of actual residence in Rhodes, and the performance of a definite number of caravans (as the voyages aboard their galleys were called), should be an absolute requirement to qualify a Knight for holding any official post or dignity whatsoever." Certainly this was a proper and wise ruling. It worked to the Order's healthy benefit then, and some such modern ruling would work most beneficially and needfully today. It is not of wisdom or servicable worth to press a round peg in a square hole, or a square peg in a round hole. While it is no difficult act to robe an illiterate and mind-stupid fellow in a king's attire, it nevertheless is impossible for such an enrobed fellow to prove his kingly worthiness.

In the passing years of Villeneuve's official incumbency, the popular story of a knight of

Rhodes slaying a hideous dragon gained credence and circulation. As the reader may be interested to read all that can be said as to the slaying, the following account is submitted. "A huge serpent, or crocodile, for it is described as an amphibious animal, had taken up its abode in a cavern on the brink of a marsh situated at the base of Mount Saint Stephen, about two miles from the city, from whence it sallied forth frequently in search of prey. Not only cattle, but even men, became its victims; and the whole island trembled at its voracity. Knight after knight, ambitious of the renown of slaying such a monster, stole singly and secretly to its haunt, and never returned. The creature was covered with scales, which were proof against the keenest arrows and darts; and at length the Grand-master held it his duty to forbid his knights from courting so unequal an encounter. Deodato de Gozon, a knight of the language of Provence, alone failed to respect this prohibition, and resolved to deliver the island from the monster, or perish. Having often reconnoitred the beast from a distance, he constructed a model of it of wood or pasteboard, and habituated two young bull-dogs to throw themselves under its belly, on a certain cry being given, while he himself, mounted and clad in armor, assailed it with his lance. Having perfected his arrangements, he bestrode his charger, and rode down privately into the marsh, leaving several confidential attendants stationed in a spot from whence they could behold the conflict. The monster no sooner beheld him approach, than it ran, with open mouth and eyes darting fire, to devour him. Gozon charged it with his lance, but the impenetrable scales turned aside the weapon; and his steed, terrified at the fierce hissing and abominable affluvium of the creature, became so ungovernable that he had to dismount and trust to his good sword and his dogs. But the scales of the monster were as proof against his falchion as his lance. With a slap of its tail it dashed him to the earth, and was just opening its voracious jaws to devour him, helmet, hauberk, spurs and all, when his faithful dogs gripped it tightly with their teeth in a vulnerable part of the belly. On this, the knight quickly sprang to his feet, and thrust his sword up to the hilt in a place which had no scales to defend it. The monster, rearing itself in agony, fell with a tremendous hiss on the knight, and again prostrated him in the dust; and though it instantly gasped its last, so prodigious was its size, that Gozon would have been squeezed to death, had not his attendants, seeing the object of their terror deprived of life, made haste to his assistance. They found their master in a swoon; but after they had with great difficulty drawn him from under the serpent, he began to breathe again, and speedily recovered. The fame of this achievement being bruited in the city, a multitude of people hurried forth to meet him. He was conducted in triumph to the Grand-master's palace; but that dignitary, heedless of popular acclamation, sternly demanded wherefore he had violated his orders, and commanded him to be carried to prison. At a subsequent meeting of the Council, he proposed that the culprit should atone for his disobedience with his life; but this severe sentence was mitigated to a deprivation of the habit of the Order. To this degradation he was forced to submit; but in a little time the Grand-master relented, and not only restored him to his former rank, but loaded him with favours."

One of Germany's greatest poets has given the literary world a magnificent poem based on this tragic story. Some have thought that the story of "St. George and the Dragon" was founded on the above, but not so, for the English myth antedated the deed of Gozon, the Rhodes knight. The historic fact is that an ancient Roman writer, Diodorus Siculus, has penned how that, centuries ere his day, Rhodes was overrun with gigantic serpents, or dragons, and that a Thessalonian warrior of fame destroyed them. This, of course, does not prove that Gozon the knight of Rhodes did not kill a dragon there. Doubtless something of this nature occurred, but the story may have been greatly elaborated. All such stories lose nothing in the on-sweep of centuries. It appears that this brave knight, Gozon, succeeded Villeneuve to the Grand-master's exalted office, and also, by many battles against corsairs on sea and Turks on land, gained great honors. He died in 1353, his name and person alike revered by all. On his upreared monument was inscribed the words, *"Here lies the Vanquisher of the Dragon."* Some time after this, the Pope intruded his authority in the realm of the Order to such a degree as caused serious fear for its continued existence. He demanded absolute and unhesitating obedience to his political plans. This autocracy conflicted with what the Grand-masters considered the duty they owed to the Order. However, as it appeared to be a clerical policy to choose an aged man for Pope, there was always the thought that a speedy change as to the Chair's incumbent would quiet matters. Frequently it was even so. Space in this Rhodian chapter will not permit any extended review as to battles fought, political controversies, property-grasping intrigues, carried on by kings and prelates. The author must hasten to set forth eventuations which ultimately compelled the illustrious Order to quit Rhodes as, centuries earlier, it quit Palestine. Toward the close of the fourteenth century the Othmanic Empire of the Turks had become vast and powerful. As to this fact, we read, "Turkey had swollen to a mighty empire, whose frontiers were the Euphrates and the Danube—the Steppes of Tartary and the Mediterranean

Sea." Bajazet the Sultan had proved himself such a warrior prince that he was nick-named, "*Ilderim*," that is, Lightning. It is authentically written of this Sultan that "it was his boast that, when he had ravaged Hungary, he would pass into Italy, plant his standard on the Capitol, and feed his war-horse with oats on St. Peter's altar." But Bajazet's boast came to naught; not, indeed, so much because he could not ultimately have thus triumphed in spite of Latin warriors, but because, in 1402, his great army came to deathly grips on the plains of Angora with the Mogul Tartar army under the superb leadership of the fearless Tamerlane. Here was fought to a finish of Bajazet one of the most terrific battles recorded in history. It ended in Bajazet being made a prisoner to die in chains. Tamerlane's host swept conqueringly through Asia Minor, and then beseiged Smyrna which was possessed by the Knights of Rhodes. On the first day of operations, Tamerlane displayed a white banner, thus signifying his readiness "to show clemency, in case of an immediate surrender. The second day, the standard was of the color of blood, signifying that the lives of the Governor and his principal officers were forfeited. But the third day, a black banner floated over the Tartar's tent; and the Christians knew that not even their voluntary submission could save them from a violent death." The writer of choice will forego any attempt to set in words the appalling scenes of slaughter which ensued ere the Tartars took the city. When an entrance was made, the in habitants were all butchered. We are told that "a few knights, and a considerable number of soldiers, however, escaped by swimming to the small craft in the harbour." Again, it appeared, as in the closing years of St. John d'Acre, as if the bell of doom was sounding the extinction of the Order of Rhodes. Yet in no past epoch of the Order's amazing history of manifold triumph and defeat had there been a time when it could marshal as many war-tested veterans as at this date. At headquarters in Rhodes there were housed permanently one thousand knights. However, it was far more a militant machine than in any charitable and primal sense a hospitallic Order. True enough, as a fighting unit it ministered to wounded men and cared for widows and orphans, for of these there was no diminishment, yet striking for new conquests, and repelling inveterate enemies, was, manifestly, its meat and drink, its chief occupation. It appears to be an universal, an immutable law, that they who live by the sword shall perish by the sword. Still, frequently enough, the clash of swords in conflict is the necessary arbitrament of injustice perpetrated.

Time and again had the fortressed city of Rhodes been vainly struck by the naval power of the Ottoman Turks, yet the enemy withdrew, if

THE WALLS OF RHODES

not defeated, yet of the mind that present effort was in vain. However, all the fortressed islands surrounding Rhodes were snatched from the knights' holding. In 1448 the last of the Emperors of Constantinople received the imperial diadem. Like that of the city's illustrious founder, his name was Constantine. Alas! his five years of sovereignty were pressed full of mind misery, for the powerful Mahomet II, the Ottoman Sultan, was intent, week by week, upon "squeezing the orange" of Constantine's holding. This Sultan, it appears, was a highly educated personage, yet very loose and licentious in his ways. Besides his native tongue, it is affirmed that he spoke or understood five languages, the Arabic, the Persian, the Chaldean, the Latin, and the Greek. He was no easy antagonist in a ruling seat of power. One ruling thought possessed his mind, viz., to possess Constantinople. The story is recorded of him that "at the dead of night, about the second watch, he started from his bed, and commanded the instant attendance of his prime vizir. The message, the hour, the prince, and his own situation, alarmed the guilty conscience of Calil Basha. On receiving the royal mandate, he embraced, perhaps for the last time, his wife and children; filled a cup with pieces of gold, hastened to the palace, adored the sultan, and offered, according to the Oriental custom, the slight tribute of his duty and gratitude. 'It is not my wish,' said Mahomet, 'to resume my gifts, but to heap and multiply them on thy head. In my turn I ask a present far more valuable and important; Constantinople.' As soon as the vizir had recovered from his surprise, 'The same God,' said he, 'who has already given thee so large a portion of the Roman empire, will not deny the remnant, and the capital. His providence, and thy power, assure thy success; and myself, with the rest of thy faithful slaves, will sacrifice our lives and fortunes.'"

In his preparations for the besiegement of the imperial city, he engaged the services of an ironmonger, a Hungarian, to mould a great cannon, capable of discharging an enormous projectile. It was, we are told, "a piece of brass ordinance of stupendous, and almost incredible, magnitude; a measure of twelve palms is assigned to the bore; and the stone bullet weighed above six hundred pounds." Constantine was not ignorant of Mahomet's preparations, and hastened to implore the Latins to come to his assistance, but little if any sincere action was taken to save the city. Religion played a neutralizing part in this contemptible indifference. It has ever been thus.

In 1453 the besiegement was on, and the fair capital of the eastern Cæsars was doomed. Space will not permit of extended remarks as to the innumerable tragic incidents which were enacted. The following brief summary must suffice. Mahomet promised a valuable gift to him who should first scale the city's defensive walls, hence we are told that "the first who deserved the sultan's reward was Hassan the Janizary, of gigantic stature and strength. With his scimitar in one hand and his buckler in the other, he ascended the outward fortification: of the thirty Janizzaries, who were emulous of his valour, eighteen perished in the bold adventure. Hassan and his twelve companions had reached the summit: the giant was precipitated from the rampart; he rose on one knee, and was again oppressed by a shower of darts and stones. But his success had proved that the achievement was possible; the walls and towers were instantly covered with a swarm of Turks; and the Greeks, now driven from the vantage ground, were overwhelmed by increasing multitudes. As to the Imperial Constantine, he was hewn down in the terrible fray, buried deeply beneath soldiers' corpses. As has been penned,—

> As to the Sovereign, let them search the field;
> And where they find a mountain of the slain,
> Send one to climb, and being down beneath,
> There they will find him at his manly length,
> With his face up to heaven, in that red monument
> Which his good sword had digged.

When Constantinople fell, to become the Capital of the Turkish Empire, no less than sixty thousand people were made captives, and the greater number of them sold to become slaves, or to suffer a more distressing doom. It is recorded that when the Sultan in person entered the carved portals of St. Sophia, the most renowned cathedral in Europe, he stood and beheld its ravished degradation, then flashed into his mind the plaintive lines of a Persian poet which he thoughtfully voiced:

The spider has wove his web in the imperial palace;
And the owl hath sung her watch-song on the towers of Afrasiab.

"Thus," writes a German, Von Hammer, "on the 29th of May, 1453, the city of the seven names, seven hills, and seven towers, was taken from the seventh of the Palaeologi (the family name of the Emperor), by the seventh Sultan of the Ottoman line." Here, then, is stated a strange numeral fact which will interest the student of the philosophy of Pythagoras.

Now we must revert our attention to Rhodes and its peerless defenders. With the Order at this crushing period it was not the thought of new conquests on land and sea, but rather the surest way to hold Rhodes as a home and sovereign possession. No labors of masonry were counted too great in order to assure of invulnerability. In truth, careful sketches of the city were drawn, and sent to the most famous engineers in Europe so that new and stouter masonry might be added to the bulwarks. Not only this, but we learn that an intelligent breed of dogs were carefully trained so as to perform scout duty. It certainly is grievous to chronicle that about this sententious period a sorry dissention occurred in the Order as to what country of the seven languages should have superior and preferential recognition as to the leading offices. The French stoutly set forth their priority claim, declaring that of the seven languages three were really of French peoples, and, besides, the first founders or Masters were Frenchmen. The heated controversy ended by the Grand-master, Zacosto, a Castilian knight, adding the kingdom of Castile to the languages. This occurred in 1461. The offices of dignity were divided among the languages as equitably as possible. As to this, we read, "The Grand-commander, who was president of the public treasury, and director of the magazines, arsenal and artillery, was taken from the language of Provence; the Marshal, who took precedence at sea, from that of Auvergne; the Grand Hospitaller, from that of France; the Admiral, from that of Italy; the Grand Conservator, from that of Aragon; the Turcopolier, or general of the horse and marine guards, from that of England; the Grand Bailiff, from that of Germany; and the Chancellor from that of Castile." In every age of mankind, honors sought after, and imposed, have been much valued by all classes and degrees of men. A consistent measure of self-consciousness as to personal importance is essential to possess, but the genuine meaure should be mentally understood. This is, however, not always the case. Many there are, devoid of intelligent wit, culture, discreet wisdom, and training, who horn and hoof for preferment and important position, yet in every degree of measurement are utterly unfitted to fill any position in the midst of their fellows, other than to be "hewers of wood and drawers of water." This class can man the bastion and the tower, but not apart from a prudent overseer. The scrub-oaks in a forest of towering, fronded pine-trees can never become in Nature's economy other species than what they are. But they can worthily grow as scrub-oaks.

Ever has it been true that in the direfulness and increasing troubles which beset a nation or community—providing always that past conduct has not filled the fateful cup of just good judgment—there appears the man who, of all men, wisely and efficiently leads and directs affairs. It was thus in the closing history of the Order of St. John in Rhodes. In 1476 there became Grand-master "one to whom we are constrained to accord the honor of being the most brilliant and the most trusted of the long line of Grand-masters—Peter D'Aubusson. In his incumbency was hurled from Rhodes a Turkish fleet of one hundred and sixty ships, after a terrific bombardment of ninety days duration. Though the Tower of St. Anthony was crumbled to pieces by prodigious guns with bores of 36 inches, yet the onslaught was stayed by D'Aubusson's masterly leadership and intrepidity. The Turks retired, leaving nine thousand corpses.

DE L'ISLE ADAM, LAST GRAND-MASTER OF RHODES

Four years later, Sultan Mahomet died, and ere dying he ordered the following inscription to be placed on his tomb, *"My intention was to have captured Rhodes and to have subjugated Italy."* But the writer must hasten his pen to inscribe Rhodes' dismal downfall, not indeed dismal as to heroic effort, but as to the Order's irreparable loss. In 1521, just sixty-eight years from the taking of Constantinople, Philip Villiers de L'Isle Adam became Grand-master. He was in France when the news of his election reached him. At once he embarked for Rhodes. Two days he had sailed when a careless seaman caused a conflagration. With herculean efforts the fire was extinguished. To the superstitious seamen the fire boded great trouble brewing. Scarcely was this mishap passed, when a tempest swept upon the ship, while a thunder-bolt struck the ship's stern, killing nine men. The same lightning shivered the Grand-master's sword blade to pieces while in its scabbard. All spoke of this as a sure omen of disaster and death. The Grand-master reached Rhodes, and soon learned that the Sultan Solyman was completing preparations to strike Rhodes with his combined naval and land forces. Never had their ensued such preparation, not even at Constantinople's besiegement. On the morning of the 26th of June, 1522, a signal from Mount St. Stephen intimated to the Rhodesians that the Turkish fleet was in sight. Four hundred sail swept past the mouth of the haven with the pomp and circumstance of a triumphant pageant; and on board this mighty fleet were one hundred and forty thousand soldiers, exclusive of sixty thousand serfs, torn from the forests of the Danube, to serve as pioneers. It appears that there was a treacherous Jew in Rhodes who wig-wagged Solyman, in some subtle way, just where to train his guns. Doubtless this infamous spy was caught red-handed, and dealt with according to his deserts. Never before in the annals of men did defenders fight with greater intrepidity and heroic persistency. The supreme limit of mental ingenuity, both by the defenders and aggressors, was reached in contriving for and against. Weeks followed weeks of incessant conflict. Bastions were smashed, huge ditches were filled with bodies, blood bespattered everything. And still the conflict raged furiously. The Sultan had vowed he would never leave Rhodes as had his predecessors, only as its possessor. For thirty-four successive nights the Grand-master lay on a pallet by the intrenchments, ready to fling himself into the strife. But why prolong the tragedy and its unspeakable horror, when the brave defenders were daily dying by hundreds, and, besides, a famine for food was weakening all the living? At last the Grand-master deemed it his Christian duty, far more painful than his personal death, to despatch deputies to the Sultan to secure just terms of surrender. Solyman received them, surrounded with Janizaries clothed in polished armour. The Sultan was ready to grant the most magnanimous terms, viz., the churches should not be profaned, no children should be taken from their parents,—every person, whether knight or citizen, should be at liberty to quit the island—that the knights should depart in their own galleys, and that they should be allowed twelve days from the ratification of the treaty, to embark their property—that their property should include relics, consecrated vessels, records and writings, and all the artillery aboard their galleys. Truly these were generous terms agreed upon! The Grandmaster was invited by the Sultan to appear in his presence, but at first hesitated, deeming it to his humiliation. However, he finally assented, and was received as a personage of highest regard by the Sultan. He requested his interpreter to console the Christian chief with the assurance that "even the bravest of men were liable to become the sport of fortune." Solyman, we are told, dismissed the venerable knight with honour; and his attendants carried back with them each a magnificent garment. Thus closed the lengthy career of the Order of St. John on the fair island of Rhodes, for on the morning of the 1st of January, 1523, the fleet, consisting of about fifty sail of all descriptions, put to sea. We will follow the knights in the ensuing chapter.

CHAPTER IX

THE KNIGHTS OF THE ORDER OF ST. JOHN AS THE KNIGHTS OF MALTA

>   A true knight,
> Nor yet mature, yet matchless; firm of word,
> Speaking in deeds, and deedless in his tongue,
> Not soon provoked; nor, being provoked, soon calmed;
> His heart and hand both open, and both free.
>   —SHAKESPEARE

TRULY, a mind torture was the wrenching away from such a charming home as the island of Rhodes. Two centuries in their passing had made the island an earthly paradise, "a thing of beauty and a joy forever." But as in Nature leaves have their time to fall, and flowers to wither, so was it as to earthly conditions with the Order of knights. The living remnant were saddened beyond words, yet with indomitable fortitude they boarded their galleys and sailed from Rhodes out upon the waters of the Great Sea, homeless indeed, yet not hopeless, for their Grandmaster was in their midst, a fortress of strength in such a depressing hour. In his soul he could ever say, "I can do all that may become a man: who dares do more is none." A fierce storm swept upon them, as if the insensate elements were in league with their home despoilers. However, storm-torn and with dismantled galleys they reached the island of Candice, a Venetian possession. Here the warriors were welcomed and invited to tarry through the winter, but the Grand-master's heart was not warm toward the authorities, for their inaction toward the Order in holding their strong fleet in home ports while Rhodes was being wrecked by the destroyer. He repaired his galleys as speedily as possible, then gave orders to the admiral of the larger ships, Austin, an English knight, to direct his course toward Sicily, while he remained with the sick and wounded aboard the smaller ships on their way to Gallipoli, on the Gulf of Tarento. The following spring the Grand-master sailed for Messina, going into port with the Order's banner furled, and in its stead a banner bearing the figure of the Virgin clasping her dead son in her arms, with the motto, "*Afflictes spes mea rebus.*" The Emperor, Charles the Fifth, invited the Grand-master to make Messina the Order's home. Charles was conscious how he had neglected to give the military help which duty demanded, and he realized that all people were convinced that he and the French King, Francis the First, were justly to blame for the Order's calamity. The Nun-Hospitallers who domiciled in Europe were greatly afflicted when they heard of the loss of Rhodes. We are told that "to mark their deep sense of the calamity that had befallen the Order, the Hospitaller-nuns, who had hitherto worn a red robe with a black mantle *à bec,* on which was a white cross, assumed a habit entirely black, in token of mourning, which they continue to wear to this day."

A deadly plague broke out in Messina shortly after the fleet's arrival, and to save his knights the Grand-master gave orders to sail away, almost distracted with multiplied troubles. The fleet put in the Gulf of Baiæ, and its human freightage encamped on the shore. In a month's passing, the plague passed away, and they sailed for Civita Vecchia, by the Pope's permission. The Pope asked for an interview with L'Isle Adam, and when the Grand-master appeared, the Pope arose and embraced him, designating him, "Hero and Defender of the Christian Faith." This indeed was very complimentary, yet as an old writer in referring to this incident, says, "Words which cost his Holiness less expense than would have done the succor necessary for the preservation of Rhodes."

The Knights were now given as an asylum the port of Viterbo, about forty miles from Rome. The Pope, it appears, was still desirous of using the Order against the infidels, hence he conversed with the Grand-master as to their securing some island home from which the knights could continue fighting the battles of the Church. In this consultation the islands of Malta and Goza were specified as the most desirable. A knightly commission was despatched to Charles the Fifth, the

Emperor of Spain and Germany, to request him urgently to give these islands to the Order as its sovereign possession. The Emperor duly listened, yet in reply gave no ready assent to the request. The truth was he desired to retain, in some politic way, authority so that he might at any time use the Order to his own advantage. Time passed, and in the meantime the Grand-master had audience with the Emperor and the King of France. As the English Language was no unimportant part and factor of the Order, when Henry the Eighth of England heard that the Grand-master was hand-in-glove with these sovereigns and had not visited his court, he forthwith voiced a demand that all English knights should give military service to his realm. This startled the Grand-master, and he speedily went to England for an audience with the King. He was received by Henry with distinction and honor. Listening to L'Isle Adam recount the Order's tragic experience, the King was deeply affected, and of willing accord rescinded the onerous measure. In leaving the King's presence, the Grand-commander was presented with "a golden basin and ewer, enriched with precious stones."

Shortly after this, the Pope and the Emperor entered into a fateful quarrel, and the powerful Emperor was excommunicated. This brought on a fierce conflict, and the soldiery of the Emperor entered Rome, compelling the Pope and his Cardinals to immure themselves in the fortress of St. Angelo. As to what occurred in the city, let a brief historic word suffice. "The streets were strewed with dead; the noblest and fairest were degraded and outraged; and the Roman blood, already contaminated with the Huns, the Vandals, and the Goths, suffered yet another pollution, from the intermingling of the Spanish and German nations." After two years of unholy strife, a reconciliation ensued between the saucy Pope and the provoked Emperor, and to show his generous feelings toward the Order of St. John, the Emperor ceded the islands of Malta, Goza, and Tripoli, to the same. As to this important enactment it is recorded as follows, "The act of donation received the imperial signature at Syracuse, on the 24th of March, 1530. By this deed, Charles ceded forever to the Grand-master and religious fraternity of St. John, in absolute title and fee-simple, all the castles, fortresses and isles of Tripoli, Malta and Goza, with the power of life and death, and that without appeal to any lord paramount whomsoever."

Thus, again, did the illustrious Order possess a home. This fact to all the knights was profoundly satisfying. Their new sovereign possession, like unto Rhodes, was wave-washed, and to men who dwelt long by the sounding sea this was extremely gratifying. Yet how different appeared the Maltese group of isles to that of the Archipelago! Still, this diverseness, by the action of the law of mind, could become an interesting factor, even a benefit. Now it will be to the reader's enlightenment for the writer to subjoin a brief historical, as also geographical lined survey of these islands. "Malta—the Melita of Scripture—lies in the bosom of the Mediterranean Sea, about fifty miles southward of Sicily, the nearest point of Europe. Its first inhabitants were of Carthaginian (Phœnician) origin (1000 B.C.), and to this day the Maltese language, which is a corrupt dialect of the Arabic, blended with Italian, is supposed to bear an affinity to the Punic (Phœnician) tongue. From the Carthaginians it passed to the Romans, who in turn gave place to the Goths, and these again to the Saracens (Arabians). In 1090 it was recovered from the Infidels by the Norman adventurers who had settled in Calabria. It afterwards became an appanage of the German Emperors, from whom it was taken by Charles of Anjou, King of Sicily, who in turn was dispossessed of it by the troops of Spain; and, after being repeatedly bought and sold for the convenience of its rulers, was finally granted to the Knights of St. John by the imperial act of donation." This brief historic survey spans no less than 2500 years in time's flight. The term, Malta, is of Phœnician extraction. It comes from the word, *Malet,* meaning a shelter, that is, a haven.

The Grand-master sent commissioners to the

islands, first of all, to secure ready-to-hand knowledge. Upon returning, the information was voiced that Malta was nothing better than "a shelterless rock of soft sand-stone called tuffa, six or seven leagues long, and three or four broad. The surface of the rock was scantily covered with earth, but of so coarse and arid a kind that grain refused to vegetate in it. It produced, however, abundance of figs, melons, and other fruits, besides cotton and cummin, which, together with honey, were exchanged by the native traders for corn with their Sicilian neighbours. The island had no rivulets, and, except in the interior, it was destitute of springs—consequently, the inhabitants had to store up the rain in cisterns. Fuel was so scarce that wood was sold by the pound; and the natives usually dressed their food on fires made with thistles and cow-dung dried in the sun. Goza was described in the same report, as divided from Malta by a channel about a league and a half wide, in the midst of which lay two islets, called Cumin and Cuminot. Goza was eight leagues in circumference, destitute of harbors, and environed by shoals and reefs, but withal blessed with a fertile soil." Certainly the commissioners' report was not of a nature to inspire the minds and jubilate the spirits of the knights. However, those unverdant isles were the possession of the Order. Of course, after the despotic manner of imperial potentates, the assent or dissent of a country's native residents, in the matter of trade or gift, had no consideration whatever. Power to possess, or, on the other hand, to dispossess, was what counted, not only with infidel monarchs, but with Christian. There was no moral—even though there were religious—distinction between them. The unbiased student is constrained to conclude thus. In passing, the writer will say that the name Goza, by which the smallest isle is designated, is derived from the old Roman word, *gaudex*, that is, a tail. As the voyager approaches the islands, the smallest isle appears like an appendix to Malta.

On October 20th, 1530, the Grand-master and his knights arrived and took possession of their new home. Just seven years had wearily passed since the day their galleys sailed away from Rhodes. Henceforward the Order was popularly known as the "Knights of Malta," and, the writer may add, will continue to exist among nations by this glory-crowned name.

Centuries before the landing of the knights in Malta, the Saracens, being then in possession, had upreared a fortress at the mouth of the great harbor. This the knights amazingly strengthened, and gave it the name St. Angelo. Opposite this gigantic granite fortress at the extreme point of a lofty and bare ridge, called Mt. Sceberras, they upreared another, almost its equal in strength, to which they gave the name St. Elmo. It was not long after the knights took possession of Malta before a project was entered into to take the city of Modon in the Morea and make it their headquarters. It appears that the Knight Prior of Rome took the leadership of this marauding expedition. Traitorous citizens of Modon were engaged, and the naval descent was made. After a sanguinary conflict was waged, the aggressors gained report that a large force was hurriedly marching to Modon's defence, and after every deed of spoiliation was perpetrated, they retreated. In this most dastardly enterprise, several hundred women were torn from their homes by the infamous Italian soldiery. Sorry to relate, some of the knights "did not scruple to share" in the spoiliation. This tragic and despicable incident much grieved L'Isle Adam, although he bore bravely up in the midst of overseeing labors. The most serious blow followed this unholy affair. One of the Prior of Rome's attendant knights quarreled with a youthful French knight and slew him. The French knights speedily moved for avengement. Soon the Italian knights and the French were clashing swords in a deadly duel. The Grand-master commanded the Prior of Rome to punish the guilty, but he, being a kinsman of the Pope, greatly more incensed the French knights by this show of favoritism. As they had cause to believe, he but added insult to injury. This, as nothing else could, wore down the spirit

THE HARBOR OF MALTA

THE NEW YORK
PUBLIC LIBRARY

ASTOR, LENOX AND
TILDEN FOUNDATIONS

of the Grand-master. Doubtless he well knew from what invidious root the trouble sprang, yet the root could not be easily uprooted without the Order experiencing more serious trouble. Many sovereigns of Europe were cognizant of this. But alas! L'Isle Adam's heart-pressing woes did not end with the tragic duel between the Italian and French knights in Malta. The King of England, Henry VIII, when but a youth was married to his brother's widow, Catharine, the daughter of the Spanish Emperor. Having become infatuated with Anne Boleyn, a lady in waiting to his spouse, Catharine, and knowing that his marital union was contrary to moral law, although it had been Pope-sanctioned on the grounds of international comity, a political affair, Henry had urged the Pope to decree his divorcement so that the unholy union might end. The Pope hesitated to grant the English monarch's appeal, for Charles had already given him humiliating proof of his anger. After three or four years of see-sawing procedure, Henry grew wrathy, and submitted the matter to an English court, the highest in the realm. The matter received a verdict as to its being null and void, hence a divorcement was granted. Hearing the issue, both the Emperor and the Pope were fiercely incensed, and Henry came under the Church's condemnation forthwith. As the English establishments of the Order of St. John were like all monastic institutions—distinctly Roman

Catholic in faith and fealty, they with all others experienced the confiscatory and dissoluting ire of stern and inflexible Henry, the real monarch of England. As this constitutes a very important factor as to the Sixth Language of the Order, the Language of and from which the American knighthood professedly springs, in this connection it is proper to submit a brief authentic statement as to Henry's dissoluting edict and action. The English historian, Camden, in his writing as to the King's action, says, "In England and Wales six hundred and forty monasteries, ninety colleges, two thousand and seventy-four chantries and free chapels, and one hundred and ten hospitals, were dissolved." Of course these summed up the total of all the various Latinized institutions in the English realm, with their tens of thousands of men and women who preferred to live apart from the hard-working citizens. They, professedly, had more religion than others, but they were not more godly. We further learn that "a bill was brought into the English parliament on the 22nd day of April, 1540, which was read a second time on the 24th, and a third time on the 26th of the same month, ordering the total suppression of the order of the Knights Hospitallers in England and Ireland; and those belonging to the various establishments were enjoined no longer to use the habit of their former titles. This bill vested in the king all the possessions of the Hospitallers, viz., their castles, honours, manors, churches, houses, mesnes, lands, tenements, rents, reversions, services, woods, underwoods, pastures, meadows, and so forth, and absolves the knights from obedience to the Pope."*

The reader will observe that the Sixth Language which was established in Scotland, being under Scotch sovereignty, did not come under this dissolving bill. As this fact will be considered and treated in the succeeding chapter, the writer will refrain here from dwelling upon it. At the time of the order's suppression in England—for which the dilly-dallying Pope was as much to blame as "Bluff King Hal,"—Sir William Weston was Knight Prior of the Order in England, with headquarters in the hospital of Clerkenwell, in London, while Sir John Rauson was Knight Prior of Ireland at Kilmainham. It was the poet Byron who wrote,

'Tis sometimes sweet to have our quarrels,
Particularly with a tiresome friend.

Certainly the Pope of Rome had tired the mind and spirit of the English king by his wig-wagging tactics,—had tired the brusque monarch, enthroned on his island, he who in his theologic dis-

* We are told that "the King of England and many great nobles enjoyed a right, called 'corrody,' of dining at the table of the Knights at Clerkenwell and elsewhere, and of this privilege they frequently availed themselves, as the Grand Prior greatly bewails in his report to Rhodes."

putation against Martin Luther, the monk of Wittenberg, was by the Holy Father designated "The Defender of the Faith." However, ecclesiastic honors and titles, like those of political imposing, have been known to go topsy-turvy, and "rip at the seams." In at least a monetary aspect, there was much sweetness came to Henry by the confiscatory procedure which his quarrel ultimated in. Just how much the Pope could credit himself in securing, the writer has no means of knowing, for notoriously is it true that Churchmen are ever scrupulously secretive as to earthly enrichments. However, obviously enough, he gained only loss in respect to England.

When the Grand-master heard of the Order's dissolution in England and Ireland from the lips of knights who exiled themselves rather than remain in England and lose their knightly status and station, his spirit was o'erwhelmed with grief, and "a violent fever deprived him of the little remains of vigour which were left him; and on the 21st of August, 1534, he expired. In him the Order lost the most illustrious Grand-master it ever possessed. His reign of thirteen years was marked by a continued succession of perils and disasters; but his bravery, his wisdom, his fortitude, his clemency, and his devotion to his Order, threw a radiance even over reverse. The knights laid him in the dust, with filial sorrow; and the simple epitaph 'Hic Jacet Virtus Victrix Fortunae'

MARSAMUSCETTO HARBOR, MALTA

(Here Lies Virtue Triumphant Over Misfortune!) was inscribed upon his tomb."

To dwell upon the multiplied and death-dealing naval warrings, and, sometimes at least, dishonorable expeditions in which the Knights of Malta took part with European troops and naval men, would be but a tragic recital of such conflicts as have been briefly outlined in former chapters, and also the rehearsal would swell the contents of this chapter to an unwarrantable degree. "Enough is as good as a feast," is as truly applicable to literary provender as to bodily need supplied. In Malta the knights of the Languages resided in separate buildings; these finely constructed edifices, in their architectural lines, distinctly marked the lineage of the various knights of the Order. It would be decidedly unjust and wrong to hold the thought that the erection of these Priory edifices bespoke unfraternity. As in Nature, "birds of a feather flock together," in like manner do the tribal and national-tongued peoples of earth prefer like association. Just here the writer may properly say, language has played a far more potent part in mankind's super-centuried drama than anything else. The hope for international peace and good-will, men toward men, depends not so much upon toadying to deep-rooted prejudices, be they religious or political, as upon a clear-minded understanding of the mind's tongued utterances. We moderns are most apt to think slightingly of the very ancient peoples of earth, but proper study will evidence to our minds that much which makes our language possible is rooted in what we term "dead languages." But such are not *dead,* nor did they ever die: they were metamorphosed. As a scholar has penned, "All the various forms of written letters now used in Europe have come in different ways from the letters first used by the Phœnicians (Philistines). The name Alphabet shows it: it comes from the first two Phœnician letters *aleph* and *beth*; in Greek, *alpha* and *beta.*" With this digression we return to our knighthood survey. We are credibly informed that the Order of Malta, for some unstated reason, inculcated a law in its statutes that no native Maltese could become a knight of the Order. Not because there were no old and aristocratic families therein, for such there were, and in every cultured way equal to Europeans, if indeed not of older distinction, as also worth. It may be that the leading knights held the thought that in time the Maltese would attain numerical preponderance, and thus control the Order's destiny. If this was the reason, it certainly was not of soul nobility. But we may well ask, when and where exists or has existed an organized body of men which has or does carry on in absolute impartiality, and that functions only and fully along the equitable line of mental and moral worth and measurement? Confessedly, the writer of this historic treatise knows not of the existence of such an institution on earth.

The Knights of Malta became almost exclusively a famed naval power, ploughing the sea with their ships of war, incessantly coming into grips with Algerian and Turkish corsair fleets. Naval improvement was ever the prime matter of consultation, and this implied artillery as well as ships. "One great ship of the Order was of enormous size, and was made shot-proof by being sheathed with iron plates." Here, then, the Order of Malta, historically, had the priority as to steel-clad ships of war. Who can safely deny that Ericson, of Monitor fame, had not in mind the iron-sheathed ship of the Knights of Malta when he caused to have built his "cheese-box"?

Though the knights of England were scattered through Europe, and housed at Malta, they still entertained the hope that the Order, subject to the Pope in religion, would be reconstructed in England and Ireland. Doubtless it is true that much secret intriguing prevailed while Henry VIII continued in life. If so, the utmost care was essential, for the King was uncompromising in word and spirit. Neither an open or prowling enemy of the king was safe in his realm. But Henry at last succumbed to death, and his daughter, Mary, by Catharine of Spain, was proclaimed Queen of England. She was in the strictest sense a devoted Roman Catholic. To her one-viewed mind, the Reformed teachings were infamous, and merited royal condemnation, and its teachers the fires of destruction, in time and eternity. Upon Mary's enthronement, one of her first official acts was to despatch an envoy to the Grand-master in Malta with the statement that "she intended to restore to the Order all the convents and estates which had been taken from it when all the English monasteries were suppressed by her father, Henry VIII." This the Queen did; but while she gave back the possessions which had become crown lands and houses, she could not persuade the nobility and others of her subjects to unloosen their purchased rights to them. It does thus appear that Mary's religious feelings were far more fervid—such as they were—than those of the Catholic nobility.

However, the Priory of Clerkenwell was re-established, in the name of Pope and Queen, for three or four terrible flesh-burning years of her none too brief reign. But Mary died, and her half-sister, Elizabeth, was crowned Queen. She saw fit to accept her royal father's law of suppression as valid, and moreover, a very necessary realm-sweeping piece of legislation. Had the English Prior of the Order studied the New Testament writings, instead of being mind-blinded by Church superstitions, the Order in the realm of Elizabeth would have been recognized, not as the Pope's weapon, but a safe and altogether worthy institu-

STRADA SAN GIOVANNI, VALLETTA

tion. Hand-in-glove with and for the Pope, it was sword-in-hand against Queen Elizabeth. Matters shifted quite differently in the Scottish Priory, as the reader will learn in the ensuing chapter.

The act of Henry VIII has been loudly and strongly condemned by the Latin Church officials in the passing centuries, but condemnation comes with poor grace from those who have persistently striven, by blood and fire, to extirpate and destroy from the earth every religious institution which is contrary to their own. Not only so, but the official letter from the Pope to King Edward II of England, against the Order of Templars in 1312, which Order had carried properly on in Edward's realm, proves how double-keyed, ruling clerics can choose to be. In the letter the Pope "commanded the King of England to seize and imprison all members of the Order on one day (as the King of France had done), and to hold in the Pope's name all the property of the Order till it should be determined how it was to be disposed of." The Pope, you see, deemed that any orders he might give were holy orders, but those which a monarch in his realm felt moved to give were unholy. But as to satisfaction, the horse that gets the oats to eat is generally the contented nag. The one law controls men and horses alike. Quite willingly does the writer pass by the years of the Order's residence in Malta and Gozo—it having lost Tripoli to the Algerians—to the year of the installation of the illustrious John de la Valette, in 1557, some twenty-seven years later. It appears that the persistent naval enterprises of the Order in Malta had shot beyond the patience of Solyman, the Turkish sovereign, and thus he determined to destroy its island stronghold. A mighty fleet, with every furnishment of destruction, soon sailed the seas westward. Valette was not ignorant of Solyman's preparation and purpose, hence he made every effort to withstand the ominous storm. He gathered around him his knights and voiced as follows, "A formidable enemy are coming like a thunder-cloud upon us; and if the banner of the Cross must quail to the unbeliever, let us remember that it is a signal that heaven demands us the lives which we have solemnly devoted to its service. He who dies in this cause dies a happy death; and, to render us worthy to meet it, let us renew at the altar those vows which ought to make us not only fearless, but invincible in the fight."

After this stirring address, he called a muster roll of his forces, and learned there were seven hundred knights with their serving-brothers, and about eight thousand five hundred soldiers, composed of the crews of the galleys, and militia. On the 18th of May, 1565, the mighty armada of the Turks hove in view. Its one hundred and fifty-nine ships carried thirty thousand fighting men, the major portion of them being janizaries,

JEAN LA VALETTE, GRAND-MASTER AT MALTA

that is, the offspring of Christian mothers who from childhood had been exclusively trained for war in the Sultan's army. They ever were his most dependable soldiery. Soon the Turkish cannon belched forth their missiles at the masonry of the fortress St. Elmo. We are told that "a battery of ten guns, each of which carried a ball of eighty pounds, two sixty pound culverins, and a basilisk of enormous dimensions, which threw stone bullets that weighed one hundred and sixty pounds, opened upon the fort." As there is a tragic sameness to every battle of blood and carnage, be it fought on land or sea, the writer of ready will refrains from penning a detailed account of this fiercely contested conflict, as some old time writers have done. However, to show the ingenuity of the military mind when confronted with a warring problem, the writer pens the following. When many Janizaries succeeded in landing, we are told that "under the Grandmaster's direction a species of fire-work was prepared, which was afterward found of infinite service in repelling the assaults. It consisted of large hoops made of wood, which, after being dipped in brandy, were rubbed over with boiling oil, and then covered with cotton soaked in a combustible preparation, two ingredients of which were gun-powder and saltpetre. This operation was repeated three times at different intervals, in order to allow each layer of cotton to cool before it was covered by another. When the hour of battle came, these hoops were set on fire, and thrown, with the aid of tongs, into the midst of the enemy. Hooped into clusters by girdles of unquenchable flame, the Turkish soldiers often lost all discipline; and, to prevent the flesh from being burned off their bones, flung themselves into the sea." How unspeakably horrible was all this! Morally considered, better far be the inventor of a sewing machine, an automobile, or even a calumet pipe of peace, than any such flesh-incinerating contrivance. However, every fateful contingency must be met and balanced by a contrivance equal to the implement or factor which endangers.

At last the strong fortress of St. Elmo fell into the hands of the Turkish soldiery, yet not until eight thousand Turks lay stark in death. The Order had lost three hundred knights and thirteen hundred soldiers. When the Turkish commander mounted the fort's bulwarks and gazed about him, it is recorded that he exclaimed, "What resistance may we not look for from the parent (meaning, Fortress St. Angelo) when it has cost us the bravest of our army to humble the child!" The sight of the heaps of Turkish corpses infuriated the Pasha, and he ordered the bodies of dead knights, headless and cross-gashed, to be tied to planks and sent adrift into the inner harbour. The taking of St. Elmo was but the beginning of the conflict, for brave Valette purposed to perish ere the Turks should possess Malta. None of Europe's princes came to his aid, not so much as the Pope's soldiery. The reader must doubtless know that the Pope at this epoch was a sovereign as well as the Papa of Christendom. At last when Valette's mind became toned with dark despair, a Sicilian fleet appeared on the horizon, and a vociferous and jubilant cheer of hope rent the air. What was to Valette's joy of heart, was to the Pasha's disturbing fears. Week after week the thunderous conflict raged, till at last, after three months and a half of horror and destruction, the Turkish fleet, leaving behind twenty-five thousand corpses of their dead, weighed anchor and compassed for its home ports. Now was there great rejoicing throughout Europe. We are told that "the Pope, boundless in his acknowledgements of the services the Grand-master had rendered to Christianity (that is, his Church), formally proffered him a cardinal's hat; but Valette rejected it as incompatible with his official duties. Philip the Second of Spain sent him, in token of admiration, a magnificent sword and poniard, the hilts of which were of gold, enriched with diamonds," We are informed that the youth of Malta today are reminded of this victorious conflict by the words of a poem printed in the local school-books. The poem concludes as follows,—

> Oh, may the story of that deathless fight
> Still make you, like your fathers, brave and strong!
> May some great minstrel shape the tale aright,
> And give it to the world in deathless song.

At the close of this memorable conflict, the Grand-master turned his excellent talent to the designing and building of a city amid the ruins and rocks of Mount Sceberras. We read, "The first great stone was laid on the point of Saint John's bulwark, and the Grand-master spread the mortar on it with his own hand. Under it were deposited a great number of gold and silver medals, on which was represented the new city, with the legend, *'Melita Renascens'*; and on the exurgue, the day and year of the foundation, 28th of March, 1566."

Some two years subsequent to this important event, Valette, as is recorded, "was struck by a *coup-de-soleil*," in other words, a sun-stroke, and soon passed into the silent tomb. As it would not be of material interest to the reader to attempt, however briefly, to recite the doings of the Malta knights throughout the many years from the heroic days of Valette in 1565 to the unheroic Grand-mastership of Ferdinand von Homspech in 1797, the writer will refrain from dwelling on the Order's existence, and movements with European powers, as those years fled by. There ensued, however, one or two incidents which the reader may be pleased to note. About the middle of the seventeenth century, Lascaris, the Grand-master, was influenced by an official Frenchman to purchase islands in the West India group, in the Western hemisphere. He bought the islands of Saint Christopher, Saint Bartholomew, Saint Croix. "The fee-simple of all these possessions, with all the plantations, slaves, and stores upon them, was purchased for about five thousand pounds sterling." Twelve years afterward the Grand-master resold them to French merchants, as they proved unprofitable to the Malta Order. Today the product of one plantation in a season brings more monied returns than the price the Order paid for the four islands.

The upheaval of the French Revolution thundered forth the end of the landed domination of the aristocrats, both secular and religious. Feudal serfdom and propertyless peasantry gave place to tillers of soil being owners of their land tillage. Soft-handed parasites who disdained all that was termed work, gave place to "Peter, Paul, and John," honorable fishermen, tradesmen, and real instructors, and respected laymen. Voracious human sharks who for centuries had swam in sleek fatness in the midst of peoples, were mercilessly arrested and their treasures of plunder redistributed. Flaring and burlesqued titles of distinction were summarily legislated into *innocuous desuetude,* or hades. Thus it was that the Knights of Malta, together with their manors, estates, and properties in France, came under the wrathful judgment of the "Republicans." The King, Louis the Sixteenth, was reduced to beggary, and the Grand-master advanced him five hundred thousand livres to procure his ransom. This political act, however estimable in itself, brought the Order into the arena of state affairs. The result was quick condemnation and confiscation. "First a decree was passed subjecting the possession of the Order to all the taxes imposed on other property—next it was enacted, that every Frenchman who was a member of any Order of knighthood that required proofs of nobility, should cease to be regarded as a citizen of France—and lastly, by an edict dated the 19th of September, 1792, the Order of Malta was declared to be extinct within the French territories, while its possessions were annexed to the national domains." We may seriously query: Was it a mere coincidence that the knights' Parisian edifice, known as the "Temple," doubtless the same edifice owned by the Templars in which Molai placed his Order's coin when he left Cyprus for Paris, was used by the citizen rulers in which to imprison the French monarch, Louis XVI. This Temple, and its rich store of money, was mercilessly torn from the Templar Knights, and the noble Grand-master burnt alive. Now a successor of Philip is placed in durance in this building, there to despairingly await guillotining. This, truly enough, is a thought-provoking reversement of persons in the

MALTA—THE OLD CITY GATES

fateful drama. The ancients would see in all this the stern and inexorable justice of Nemesis!

The Order was still existent in Malta; but not for many days, for the world-ambitious Napolean Bonaparte, the militant genius, had far reaching schemes of conquest. Ferdinand von Hompesch was the first and only German that became Grandmaster. Under his leadership the Emperor of Russia was appealingly asked to become officially "Protector of the Order." He accepted the high-sounding title, together with "a superb coat of mail, and a jewelled cross, the possession of heroic La Valette. While all this was going on, the first division of Napoleon's Republican fleet was on its way for Malta. On the 6th of June, 1798, it reached the islands. Where was the new-made imperial Protector? Napoleon doubtless smiled at the performance of his induction into office. Three days later Napoleon appeared with his grand fleet, and demanded immediate entrance into the inside harbor of Malta. It is needless to say that Napoleon's demand was assented to. His troops were quickly landed, and the Republican Admiral, with his officers, followed. The movement was more of a parade than aught else. As the famous Admiral with expert eye viewed the granite fortresses he turned to one of his officers, and said, "It is well, General, that there was some one within to open these gates to us. We should have had some trouble in entering if the place had been altogether empty." Napoleon's command was that all knights should quit the island forthwith. "About ten pounds sterling was advanced to each knight for the expenses of his journey, but he was not permitted to depart until he had torn the cross, the emblem of the Order, from his breast, and mounted the tri-coloured cockade." Not only was this suffered by the aristocrat knights, but the Grand-master "was not even allowed to carry with him the archives of the Order. All the Republican rapacity consented to spare, were a part of the true cross, which the knights had brought with them from the Holy Land; the hand of St. John, presented by the Sultan Bajazet to the Grand-master D'Aubusson; and a miraculous image of the Holy Virgin of Philerme." Of course, such a genius as Napoleon failed utterly to appraise the religious value, or, indeed, genuineness, of these relics. A mortal must be peculiarly minded to appreciate such things. To conclude the dramatic ending of Malta knighthood, it will be of interest to the reader to learn that "the standards and trophies of the Order were all carried away by the spoilers; but these relics never reached the country for which they were destined. Part of them perished in the *Orient*, the French flag-ship, which was blown up in the memorable battle of Aboukir; and the rest were captured by the English in the *Sensible* frigate, which shortly after fell into their hands."

After the French naval power was shattered by that of the British under command of Admiral Nelson, Malta was closely blockaded for two trying years ere the French General assented to surrender. As it was suicidal to maintain his stubbornness longer, on September the 4th, 1800, he yielded Malta to General Pigot, and thus Malta became a part of the British Empire. Today the Maltese would not have it otherwise. Strictly speaking, the Order of Malta became extinct, as far as any residence in Malta was concerned. Yes, in a more definite manner than in England in the reign of Elizabeth, for although as an Order it was dissolved in England, all its members were not driven out of the realm, although unrecognized as such. However, the whole of the Sixth Language was not extinct, for the Scottish Priory still carried on, as the reader will be told in the ensuing chapter, as also in what measure and manner the Order has undergone transformation and rejuvenation. Thus it is that much that will be of especial interest to the up-to-date reader is set forth in the following chapter.

CHAPTER X

THE SIXTH LANGUE OF ENGLAND, SCOTLAND, AND IRELAND: ITS DISSOLUTION AND RESUSCITATION; AS ALSO A REVIEW OF THE ESTABLISHMENT OF THE ORDER IN AMERICA

"Oh, hallowed memories of the past,
Ye legends old and fair!
Still be your light upon us cast,
Your music on the air."

HAVING perused the previous chapters of historic review, the reader has mentally wafted down the stream of the Order of St. John to the point in its coursing when, by the despotic action of sovereign rulers, it swept, as an international organization, into the murky gulf of inaction. As an accredited sovereign Order it came to its end in England in 1559, and its landed possessions and edifices became state properties. Thus it was that the Sixth Langue went into dissolution some 233 years prior to that of the French sovereignty in the reign of Napoleon Bonaparte, that is, in 1792.

Now as it is set forth on the printed page by some present day writers that the Sixth Langue of the ancient Order never ceased to "carry on," but preserved itself intact through the years of becloudment to the present day, not in England, but in Scotland, it becomes the important duty of the author of this treatise to unveil, as completely as he is able, the authenticity and validity of this Scottish claim. If it be clearly valid, every accoladed Sir Knight will have cause to be glad; if otherwise,—well, he will be compelled to consider knightly honors from a different view point than that of ancient chartered rights, of official succession. All in all, the latter may equal in living value the former. It is as to valuation a matter of mind.

However, it will be of interest, and also enlightenment, to scan carefully all historic ground relating to the matter of the Sixth Branch of the octaved Order of St. John.

The definite year date of establishment in England is not set down, yet the following lines from the pen of George Thomas Beatson, M. D., C. B., author of *The Knights Hospitallers of Scotland, and Their Priory at Torphichen,*—which is a valued work—will assist our minds. He writes, "I have mentioned that it was about 1100 A.D. that the English Langue or Province of the Order was established in London, and that it soon became very prosperous . . . Consequently, it is not surprising that a settlement of the Order was made in Scotland in 1124 A.D., at a time when conditions for such a step were exceptionally favourable." This establishment date in London gives twenty-four years' priority to England. It is consistent to believe that the English Langue took its name from the place or kingdom in which it was first established. It appears that the Order existed in England some eighty-five years before the Grand Priory of Clerkenwell, London was founded. This occurred in 1185 A.D. Now as to the founding of the Scotish Priory at Tophichen, there is no date set down. Sir Thomas H. Gilmour, in his book, *Knights of Malta; Ancient and Modern*, writes,—"we have it on record that Archibald, Magister of Torphichen, held the office of Grand Prior in 1252." This, the reader can see, was sixty-seven years subsequent to the founding of the English Priory. It is authentic history that James Sandilands was the last Scottish Prior of Torphichen Priory. He was installed Prior in 1547 and died in 1596. While England and Scotland were two sovereignties, the two Priories were one in spirit and code. As the Sixth Langue they could not be otherwise, for the Order was one. This is a point which some writers have ignored; but it is important. King Henry VIII, as we have stated in the preceding chapter, formally dissolved the Order in England and Ireland in 1540 A.D., bringing to an end the Grand Priory of Clerkenwell. This was a fatal blow to the Sixth Langue, both in England, Ireland, and Scotland. Twenty-seven years prior to this dissolution, the Scottish army had been utterly defeated by the English king's army on Flodden Field. Both the Scottish King and his son were slain. Scotland in this way came under the power of the English throne, hence, as the reader can understand, the Priory of Torphichen became subject to the will of the English monarch. Not only this, but the Scottish Prior, James Sandilands, became a devout Protestant some five years from the date of his installation. As the Order was a confessed Roman Catholic institution it was quite impossible for Sandilands to function as Prior when Mary Stuart was hailed as Queen. She, of course, was a Catholic. As to the action taken by Sandilands, we read,—"he went at the request of the Grand Priory to hand over to the Queen the lands and possessions of the Order, together with the dignity of the Lord St. John, which he held as chief of the Order." This action, clearly enough, brought an ending to the Scottish Priory. From this event onward there did not exist in Scotland a legally recognized Order of St. John. The reader may inquire, what was the date of this action? The date is not stated, but we may approximate the time. Mary was proclaimed Queen in 1542, and she died in 1567. Within these twenty-five years the date falls. Sandilands lived twenty-nine years after the Queen died. It is both unauthentic and inconsistent to hold that the Order continued on in Scotland subsequent to this action. If there existed a scrap of documentary evidence as proof that it did so, in a clandestine, that is, secret way, as Mr. Gilmour in his book intimates it did, such a scrap has not been set forth by any historian. Mere personal opinion does not make fact in any case. We can generously respect a man's stated belief, be it right or wrong, but we do him no injury when we choose to decide his opinion carries no weight of established fact. When Mr. Gilmour writes, "The Order continued to exist (in Scotland), and whether Lord Torphichen (Sandilands) continued to hold the office of Grand Prior or not, he positively did continue to be a leader in the Protestant cause, where he led the same men as he led in the grand Prior," he pens no authentic statement, but his personal opinion. How much more consistent and creditable are the following lines from the pen of Sir Richard Brown, Bart., who for twenty years was the Grand Secretary of the modern English Langue of St. John. He writes, "After flourishing in the British Islands from the year of our Lord 1104 to 1566, the venerable Langue of England merged, owing to extended violence, in the general body of the Order, and it emerged from the same in 1831, by virtue of the sovereign authority vested by a majority of the constituent Langues in the Capitular Commission of Paris." In the body of this statement we have historic fact inwritten. It is not personal opinion in printed dress. This gentleman makes use of the word "merge" in relation to the condition of the English Branch of the Order from 1566 to 1831. What does the term mean? In the

Standard dictionary the term is defined as follows: "'To sink the identity or individuality of; cause to disappear, be combined, or be swallowed up; to be absorbed into something else." Now such was the state and experience of the Sixth Langue of the Order. However, it emerged anew in a modernized dress in 1831, and is today carrying on a hospital and ambulance work both in England and Scotland. This is provable and approved fact.

But the above historic fact is wholly—however unwarrantably and unjustly—brushed aside and ignored by our Scottish confreres who prefer to claim definitely an unbroken knighthood succession from the Priory of Torphichen. No authentic documents are shown to verify and substantiate this claim, so far as the author of this treatise can discover. It is set forth on printed page that in a session of the "Grand Black Chapter of Ireland" in 1850, a Committee reported as follows, "The Order never was dissolved and that they held the chain of transmission which was perfect in all its links." The author of *Knights of Malta*, Mr. Gilmour, writes of this as being "authoritative," but why and in what way he does not state. We might reasonably ask: from what knightly source *emerged* the Grand Black Chapter of Ireland? Also, when and in what manner did it come into credentialed powers? If in truth it was *perfectly* linked with the Order of St. John of the old Priory of Torphichen, it certainly would not be asking too much to show the chain's interlinking. From *History of the Ancient and Honorable Fraternity of Free and Accepted Masons*, 1891 edition, we subjoin the following. "Long after the Reformation, when the Hospital and Templar lands in Scotland were ceded to the British Crown, independent bodies sprang up under the name of 'Knights Templars of St. John of Jerusalem,' attached to the Masonic Fraternity and who, toward the end of the last century erected Grand Masters or Grand Commanderies of their own ... It is impossible that they could be the representatives of the chivalric Order of Malta, which continued there until the surrender of the Island in 1796, and had issued edicts of expulsion against the members of the Scottish branch of St. John as unfaithful to their vows." It may be a disappointment to the reader to have the author of this treatise pen the fact that no information of valid worth has been gleaned by him. Mere statements, unsubstantiated by documentary evidence, do not create fact. From all sources of information which the writer has vised, much could be set forward which would, doubtless, make interesting reading, but assuredly would not be inspirational, and perhaps not mind cheering to the reader. The writer pens not as a judge, but as an historic reviewer and searcher of facts. In this sense, and in none other, his confessed inability is tabulated. The writer is not unmindful of the psychological fact, known to all students of that science, that what may be accepted by one man as well-founded fact, may, and frequently is, considered by another as utterly unworthy of credence or acceptance. This is why documentary evidence is essential to verify a claim. Now no reasonable mind will doubt the existence of knights, both of St. John Hospitallers and Templars, in Scotland subsequent to the ending of both fraternities. The reader may rest assured that such was the case. Not only so, but that in some silent and private way they preserved knighthood. This was, however, as true of English knighthood as of the Scottish and Irish. If there had not been English knights of St. John living in 1831 A.D. how could the English Langue "emerge" into a renewal status, as officially stated? Had there existed no knights, duly and truly accoladed, the Paris sessional action would have been a creation, not a revival of the old Order. However, Mr. Gilmour in his historic treatise manifestly enough disrelishes the thought as to the Order of St. John being in a state of abeyance from Sandilands' day to these modern times, for he writes, "That the Order continued in a publicly recognized manner is shown by the fact that about the year 1572 David Seaton with a portion of the Scottish Knights separated themselves from the then Protestant fraternity. He retired to Germany where he died in 1591, the remnant of the Seceders ultimately finding a shelter under the wing of the first lodge of Scottish Masons at Kilwinning, Ayershire, where they introduced the Orders of St. John, which are still given in connection with (Blue) Masonry." Now to the mind of the writer the contents of all this clearly discloses a complete disintegration, a final breaking to pieces of all that constituted the Scottish Branch of the Order. No authentic facts are appended to show that any publicly official portion of the Order remained and carried on. In such a light the writer sums it up. The Order in Scotland, as in England, ceased to exist as such, legally and socially.

From what *detritus* came into substantial and organic construction the modern Fraternity of Knights of Malta, vigorously carrying on in this nation, the writer of this review possesses no clear informing word to submit. Doubtless there existed in Scotland, as in other countries, both knightly matter and accoladed men throughout the period of what has been termed "abeyance," that is, a state of suspension, of inaction. As to who the men were, and from whence they secured the furnishments by which a reconstruction has ensued, has not been clearly set forth, so far at least as the writer has learned. However, the work has eventuated, and the modernized Order is helpfully functioning. Sir Knights of American citizenship can serviceably go forward accomplishing knightly duties, and by so doing make to their Order of Malta a name as worthy as that of the Order "in days of old when knights were bold, and barons held their sway." In these thrilling years of quickly outwrought, and essentially new departures in every realm of human activity, as the writer views it, it would not comport with the times to hug closely to what in the parlance of Orders is fondly termed, "the old land-marks." To be iron-glue sticklers, real musty conservatives, in this regard, only works to deadness. As leaves have their Nature-decreed time to fall and wither, so institutions must be elastic enough to stretch to current conditions. So long, therefore, as an Order retains as a working factor those humane, virtuous, and men-serving principles, deathless in their Heaven-honoring nature, it can properly carry on even through great changes in mode and dressing prevail. This statement of the writer, as the reader can well discern, freely and fully applies the healing balm to all unhistoric lapses, weaknesses, deficiencies, errors, and what not, which may, or may not be considered ailments in and of our American Order's inalienable heritage from antiquitous years. In the last analysis it is a vital fact that those Scottish gentlemen —were they few or many—who brought across the billowy Atlantic the constituted substance, the amazingly rich and varied furnishments and degreed codes which go to the make-up of what is known as the Order of the Knights Hospitallers of St. John, Rhodes, and Malta, have earned every American Knight's heartiest and life-lasting thanks. The writer goes farther in saying that the founders fully merit from Malta Knighthood in America some special and substantial recognition, generously bestowed, which would comport with our mutual appreciation of the firmly established Order. As an historical reviewer the writer, without fear or favor, endeavored to probe into and uncover facts. All this research was wholly, and properly, apart from his estimate and appreciation of the splendid work accomplished in our changing times. No broken or lost "link" in an Order's chain of years affects in the least degree either the living reputation or character of any member of the Order. Moreover, in the last analysis, the outliving of the member is of preeminent importance.

It is in these United States of America that the Order of Malta, as in no other nation, is encouragingly growing. From 1868 to 1884, some sixteen years, we find from the Imperial Encampment's Report, that there were eight Commanderies in our nation in working status. Quite in accord with the initial history of every institution among men, dissatisfaction, confusion, and sidestepping gained currency. The deplored fact brought about the holding of a Council in the city of Philadelphia, upon June 1st, 1889. The Imperial Encampment of Glasgow, Scotland, was represented at the Council by Sir Robert Stewart, the Past Imperial Assistant Grand Master. All matters bearing upon the disaffection were carefully considered and amicably and satisfactorily adjusted, and an "Agreement of Union" was formulated and duly signatured. Since the date of this important session, the Order in this nation has been able to tabulate very pronounced progress, while its outlook towards greater achievement was never so propitious as at the present hour. From the Report of the Supreme Commandery for 1921, the number of working Commanderies in the United States is tabulated at 356. This, the reader can observe, is a remarkable advancement since the date of the Agreement of Union. The first Grand Commandery was instituted in the year 1893. Up to date there are six chartered Grand Commandery jurisdictions. The following list is explanatory as to dates of institution, as also States:

Grand Commandery of Pennsylvania	Nov. 18, 1892
New Jersey	Jan. 3, 1893
Massachusetts, Rhode Island, and Connecticut,	Oct. 17, 1895
Maine and New Hampshire	Sept. 15, 1904
New York	Dec. 1, 1904
Ohio	Jan. 10, 1920

Numerically considered, the State of Pennsylvania is the banner State. As to membership, this State has greatly outdistanced all others, and there manifestly is no slowing down to accommodate the slower advancements of other jurisdictions. However, this deer-hound speeding breeds no fret or jealousy in the spirits of other State bodies of Sir Knights, but rather fraternally stimulates, and is a source of mutual satisfaction, for the reason that the Order is a unit in purpose and spirit. Still, as the expanding work is today visualized, the stalwart banner State will do well to look to its champion banner, for a significant momentum in other jurisdictions is in the air, and remarkable results are the order of the day.

The American Branch of the Order of Knights Hospitallers of St. John, Rhodes, and Malta, has cause to rejoice that it "carries on" altogether apart from the clamor and invidious contention which, obviously, obstructs and in much tends to nullify the influence of the Order in other countries. No question of priority rights hinders and maims the Order in America. And, we may intelligently query: Of what human or earthly importance practically considered, is the thought or problem of priority? If a bushel of apples has been picked a week or two earlier than another bushel, providing the apples in both the one and the other are sound and juicy, wherein is the distinctive and preferential difference as to choice? Even though the two bushels should bear labels designating that they did not grow in the same orchard, providing they are similar fruit and altogether sound and luscious, would it not be proof of silliness to reject the one because the fruit-bearing trees grew not in the same field? There has been penned a statement by the historian, Sir Richard Brown, Bart., which to the writer tones a living truth, a truth well worthy of every Sir Knight's hearty acceptance. He writes, "The cross of St. John, when not worn as a bauble, but as an outward sign of an earnest Christian purpose, is as sure a symbol of the true and sole nobility as patriot or philanthropist can aspire to wear. The chivalry of the Order of St. John is not the bastard chivalry which prides itself in collars and ribbands, jewels and stars; but the chivalry whose religion is that of faith, hope, and charity, carried into all the relations and habits of daily life."

The estimate of value as generally placed to the credit or discredit of an Order, may, and often is, incorrectly placed. It is the character factor and status of members of the Order which determines the valuation, not the constitutional code and fabric which has made the Order possible. Weed-upspringing in a field of excellent soil is a deplorable eventuation, but the fact does not properly evidence the ground's uselessness or cheapness. Weeds implant and germinate in all fields, and it is for those who oversee and work the fields to outroot them to the soil's honor and the field's fruitfulness. It is well to know that a censorious critic outside or in the Order which he chooses to berate, is not one iota better in mind and disposition than those who make up its membership. The primal question is this: To what end and for what purpose does the order function? Also, is it properly equipped to justify the hope that it can accomplish the high aim it has in view? True enough, membership timber of the proper quality is a necessary factor to substantial results, especially so as to the men who are recognized and are its officials. However praiseworthy an automobile may be in its mechanical construction, if an ignorant driver has control of its wheel and levers, there is serious reason to think of little else than wreckage. Now in the light of such reasoning the Order of Malta in America in an admirable manner stands the test. Its purpose and aim is a man-ennobling one; its furnishments are second to no other organic institution on earth; its Commanderies are composed of substantial and intelligent American citizenry. All in all, from whatever view point it is examined, it sums up a most excellent institution, freely worthy of public recognition and esteem.

Of course, it is not for the writer of this treatise to unveil to the reader's mind the interesting warp and weft of the mind-instructive degrees which comprise the ritualistic fabric of the Order. Such knowledge is alone for its knightly members. However, it can be stated that no Christian man

THE SCOTTISH WARRANT

will find aught else inwoven into the ritualistic garmenting but that which is in acceptable blend and accord with the Sacred Text, the Holy Scriptures. While confessedly it is unknowing to the author of this treatise as to when, by whom, or where the degrees originated, as there are no writings that make it known, this lack of knowledge in no way militates against their composition, or robs them of their beauty and intrinsic value. The serviceable value of a thing depends not upon its having the stamp of past centuries upon it. If it befits living men, and in every way goes to minister to a real need, it is of useable worth. Malta's degrees measure up in every way to knighthood conditions, mentally, morally, and fraternally.

Granted that it is a fact that what are denominated "the old land-marks" are ill-defined, almost obliterated, and most difficult to discern, the present fact that such an Order exists and functions, possessing every furnishment essential to modern knighthood, is sufficient to satisfy the average man. The mortal who is extremely exacting as to non-essential points is living in close kinship with the cynic, and is more a despoiler than aught else.

The militant phase of the old knighthood orders is preserved, measurably, at least, in the fraternities of our times, especially those which claim kinship with the battling orders of crusading times. Both the Malta Sir Knights and the Templars memorialize their parentage by donning on public occasions very showy uniforms. Inherently in man is a love for expressive garmenting. As to woman possessing the more o'erbounding passion for showy apparel, is questionable. Of willingness the writer leaves this controversial matter for others to dwell upon. Undoubtedly it is true that the dressing of the soldier plays a drawing part in gaining recruits for militant duties. This tendency has been noted, and influentially used, in every age of mankind. Not alone uniforms are attractively worn by members of knighthood bodies, but an ostentatious displayment of badges, jewels, braidings, and so forth, go to personal decoration. Perhaps in no other way is self-consciousness and the readiness to be looked upon as of elevated worth, so conspicuously outwritten than in this manner. However, as it is a harmless vanity, and goes to brighten up what otherwise might be gauged as dull and unattractive, it all goes to serve a purpose, it may be, a need. Not a vestige of militant thought or purpose is now related to existent knighthood, at least not to the orders which voice the names of St. John of Malta and the Templars; hence it follows that the designation, knight, as modernly used, from the stand-point in which it was used in olden years, is a misnomer. However, words change their meaning in the coursing of time. Truly, no substantial loss has ensued by the lapse of militarism in connection with these orders of knighthood. Would that it were possible for all nations of earth to reforge their weapons of war—all of them—into virtuous tools of industry and agriculture! Militarism ever and in every nation is a hideous and burdensome evil, however much showy pageantry is attached to it, and certain dispositioned men prefer the public distinction it brings them. Wherein is the ennobled honor, one may ask, in attaining expertness in human slaughtering? Still, this constitutes but one phase—the horrid one—of the profession. To shield and preserve, while o'erwhelming the antagonist, is a vital part of the game of blasting war.

> "One to destroy, is murder by the law;
> And gibbets keep the lifted hand in awe;
> To murder thousands, takes a specious name,
> War's glorious art, and gives immortal fame."

Knights much prefer war's piercing weapons in repose, not in resistless action. To them they but symbolize Heaven's law of justice and equity. If it be contended that weapons accomplish this in bloody strife, it can be replied: where and when has ensued a fierce and deathly conflict in which the leaders and instigators of both armies did not consider their contention was clearly for justice and honor? Man slaying—and ever the offenceless—is not justice administered, but hate in horrid infliction. Modern Knights are to be commended for their fraternal transformation of war's weapons and wearing apparel. If military lords could be constrained to do likewise, earth's war-torn peoples might heartily rejoice, and infamous burdens be cast off.

In concluding our review of stirring episodes in bygone centuries, especially those in which the brave Knights of St. John and the Knights of the Temple participated and were, indeed, the prominent factors, to the reader it may appear that no distinct proof has been penned as to an unbroken lineage existing between the present day orders of St. John of Jerusalem, Rhodes, and Malta, and Knights Templars, and the ancient fraternities of those names. Distinctly no: yet in some correlative degree and manner there is much in the fabric which is declarative of relationship. The present day orders, as they are fashioned, could not have upsprung had there been no ancient root and trunk from which to grow. They have out-sprung from derivative orders, even though the parental derivatives had gone into dissolution, as history sets forth. Dissolution is by no means annihilation. To illustrate, there could not have been much or any of the hewn timber, prepared by Solomon, inserted in the rebuilt Temple which was built upon the ruins of the original edifice. Such a mechanical, rather, material fact, in no way militated against the latter as being the Temple.

The rebuilt edifice was not a counterfeit structure. Whether, then, much or little of what made up the organisms of the old orders had been inserted in the rehabilitated ones of today, is not a vital matter. These two orders exist among men as the functioning exponents of the choicest principles of what characterized the virtuous greatness of the Knights of St. John Hospitallers, and the Knights Templar. Membership in the one or the other will attest the truth of this statement. Cynics and unknowing babblers may continue to cut their swaths in the field of contentious debate, but the one who visualizes aright will clearly know they have but scythed the embittered weed crop of their own minds.

A NATION'S TRUE STRENGTH
By W. Henry Lannin

What makes a nation great?
Not enmassed hosts in glint of war,
Nor steel-clad ships with rifled spar,
And turrets fevering for their prey,
In naval pomp and war's array;
Not mints that press and stamp pure gold,
Nor luxury living men, proud, bold;
Not enstored goods in city hive,
Possessed by traders who contrive,
By advertising scheme and plan,
To sell to buyers, business fan;
Tis true, men term such nation strong,
But to one mind, at least, they're wrong.

A nation's strength is summed up true,
By moral fibre, what's just, true,
Enthroned, ingrained in heart and mind,
Of men who are not conscience blind;
Who virtue own though coin be rare,
Who truth outlive, with others share;
Who daily master base desires,
Who're ever honest, are not liars;
Who open souls to all that's fair,
Will damage none a weight of hair;
Such men endecked on ship of State,
Do ever make a nation great.

Words change their meaning as time flies;
Truth's often wounded, never dies.
Thus strength is twisted to suit mould
Of worshippers of self, of gold;
Yet, as the planets swing in spheres,
Astounding great through passing years,
Men's thoughts, though concaved from straight line,
Return to truth, behold it shine.
Like brain with opium fumes accursed,
Men dream of riches, court gold first;
Count strength by coin that's owned in till,
To wake at last from falsehood's pill.

AUTHORITIES STUDIED AND CITED

Boisgelin's History of Malta (2 vols.), London, 1805.
The Achievements of the Knights of Malta, (2 vols.), by Alexander Sutherland, Esq.
Memoir of the Illustrious and Sovereign Order of St. John of Jerusalem, by Robert Bigsby, LL.D.
A History of the Knights of Malta, (2 vols.), by Major Whitmore Porter.
Malta and the Knights Hospitallers, by Rev. W. K. R. Bedford, M.A.
Knights of Malta, Ancient and Modern, by Sir Thomas H. Gilmour.
History of the Popes, (3 vols.), by Archibald Bower, Esq.
Decline and Fall of the Roman Empire, (4 vols.), by Edward Gibbon.
Coins of the Grand Masters of the Order of Malta, by Robert Morris, LL.D.
The Chair of Peter, by Count Murphy.
History of England, (5 vols.), by David Hume.
Encyclopedia Britannica: "Arts," "Malta," "Crusades," "Knights of the Temple."
History of France, by Eyre Evans Crowe.
Synoptical Sketch of the Illustrious and Sovereign Order of Knights Hospitallers, by Hon. Sir Richard Brown.
Buried Cities Recovered, by Rev. Frank S. DeHass D.D.

AUTHORITIES

History of Knights Templars, by Mr. C. G. Addison.
Vertot's Knights of Malta, (2 vols.), London, 1728.
History of Knighthood, (2 vols.), by Hugh Clarke, 1784.
Military Religious Orders, by F. C. Woodhouse, M.A., London, 1879.
The History and Antiquities of the Round Church, by William Wallen, F.S.A.
Malta, by Frederick W. Ryan.
The Knights Hospitallers in Scotland, by George Thomas Beatson, M.D., C.B.
History of the Ancient and Honorable Fraternity of Free and Accepted Masons, 1891.
Historical Landmarks of Free Masonry, by Rev. G. Oliver, D.D., 1858.

IMPORTANT HISTORIC DATES

Solomon's Temple dedicated	B.C. 1005
Temple destroyed by King Nebuchadnezzar	610
Temple rebuilt	519
Jerusalem rebuilt	445
Jerusalem in hands of Romans	63
The crucifixion of Jesus	A.D. 34
Jerusalem destroyed	70
Jerusalem rebuilt	117
The emperor Constantine converted	325
Order of St. Lazarus founded	370
The Roman Empire divided	476
Mohammed born in Mecca	571
Mohammed's Hegira	622
Jerusalem taken by Omar the Arabian	637
Jerusalem given to Charlemagne	799
Amalfi merchants build hospital in Jerusalem	1048
Crusade army besieges Jerusalem	1099
Godfrey chosen as Christian King	1099
Clerkenwell Hospital founded	1101
Hospitallers become Knights of St. John	1118
Raymond du Puis chosen Grand Master	1118
Order of Knights of the Temple founded	1119
Order of St. John introduced into Scotland in the reign of the Scottish king, David I	1124
Founding in Scotland of Priory Torphichen	1153
Dames of the Hospital left Jerusalem	1180
Clerkenwell Priory, London, England, built	1185
Jerusalem taken by the Turkish army	1187
Richard Cœur de Lion of England a crusader	1189

260 IMPORTANT HISTORIC DATES

Germanic Order of Knights founded	1192
Jerusalem recaptured by the crusaders	1228
Recaptured by the Turkish army	1244
Knights of St. John repair to Cyprus	1290
Knights of the Temple repaired to France and arrested	1310
Order of Templars dissolved by royal decree	1310
Order of St. John capture island of Rhodes	1310
Jacques de Molai, Templar, burnt at stake	1312
Clerkenwell burnt by the rebel, Wat Tyler	1380
Constantinople taken by the Turkish army	1453
Clerkenwell rebuilt	1504
Rhodes torn from the St. John Knights	1523
Grand Master de Lisle Adam receives deed of Malta	1530
English Branch suppressed by King Henry VIII and all properties confiscated	1540
Scottish Branch dissolved under the administration of Prior John Sandilands	1547-1596
Malta seized by Napoleon and Order dissolved	1798
Malta captured by British from French	1800
Renewal of the Order in England by authority of the Capitular Commission held in Paris, France	1827
Queen Victoria granted Royal Charter to Order	1840
Scottish charters issued for American Commanderies	1870
American Supreme Grand Commandery chartered	1889